ISSUES THAT CONCERN YOU

Our Climate Future

Martin Gitlin, *Book Editor*

GREENHAVEN
PUBLISHING

Published in 2018 by Greenhaven Publishing, LLC
353 3rd Avenue, Suite 255, New York, NY 10010

First Edition

Articles in Greenhaven Publishing anthologies are often edited for length to meet page requirements. In addition, original titles of these works are changed to clearly present the main thesis and to explicitly indicate the author's opinion. Every effort is made to ensure that Greenhaven Publishing accurately reflects the original intent of the authors. Every effort has been made to trace the owners of the copyrighted material.

Library of Congress Cataloging-in-Publication Data

Names: Gitlin, Marty, editor.
Title: Our climate future / Martin Gitlin, book editor.
Description: First edition. I New York : Greenhaven Publishing, [2018] I
  Series: Issues that concern you I Audience: Grade 9 to 12. I Includes
  bibliographical references and index.
Identifiers: LCCN 2017032282 I ISBN 9781534502246 (library bound) I ISBN
  9781534502840 (paperback)
Subjects: LCSH: Climatic changes--Juvenile literature. I Climatic
  changes--Social aspects--Juvenile literature. I Climatic changes--Effect
  of human beings on--Juvenile literature. I Climatic changes--Political
  aspects--Juvenile literature. I Global warming--Juvenile literature.
Classification: LCC QC903.15 .O87 2018 I DDC 304.2/50112--dc23
LC record available at https://lccn.loc.gov/2017032282

Manufactured in the United States of America

Website: http://greenhavenpublishing.com

CONTENTS

The year was 1712. British industrialist Thomas Newcomen invented the first widely used steam engine, thereby laying the groundwork for the Industrial Revolution and popularization of coal on an industrial scale. Little could anyone have imagined that the development would lead three centuries later to a debate about climate change and the very survival of the planet.

Other environmental landmarks throughout history have provided warnings to humankind that their actions were taking a toll. As long ago as 1824, French physicist Joseph Fourier coined the term "greenhouse effect" to describe changes in the Earth's temperature. In 1900, soon after Karl Benz unveiled the Motorwagen, generally regarded as the first automobile, Swedish chemist Knut Angstrom claimed that carbon dioxide (CO_2) emissions into the atmosphere absorb parts of the infrared spectrum, leading to the conclusion that it causes warming.

The first definitive proof of climate change resulted from the exhaustive work of British engineer Guy Callendar, who utilized 147 weather stations throughout the globe in 1938 to show that the temperature worldwide had indeed risen over the previous century, as had CO_2 concentrations. But what became known as the "Callendar Effect" was generally refuted by meteorologists.

Ongoing research finally motivated a presidential advisory committee in 1965 to admit that the greenhouse effect was a legitimate concern. The term "global warming" was coined by US scientist Wallace Smith Broecker in 1975. Two international treaties, the Montreal Protocol (entered into force in 1989) and the Kyoto Protocol (entered into force in 2005), resulted in agreements to reduce emissions that damage the ozone layer. Meanwhile, global temperatures rose at an alarming pace. According to the National Aeronautics and Space Administration (NASA) and the Goddard Institute for Space Studies (GISS), the 10 warmest years globally over the last 136 have all occurred since 2000, with the exception of 1998. The year 2016 ranked as the warmest. The studies concurred with those taken by the Climate Research Unit and the National Oceanic and Atmospheric Administration.

Yet despite the evidence, carbon emissions from the burning of fossil fuels continued to rise, reaching eight billion tons per year in 2006. China overcame the United States as the biggest offender in greenhouse emissions in 2009, but the latter remained on top of the dubious rankings on a per-capita basis. Meanwhile, the rise in ocean levels due to added water from melting land ice and the expansion of sea water as it warms have also provided cause for grave concern.

Many believe the number and ferocity of natural disasters such as tsunamis and hurricanes in recent years have been the result of climate change. NASA has acknowledged that climate change might not be the cause of the disturbing increase in such weather-related events, but the organization did warn of its future impact. It cited the Panel on Climate Change, which stated that an increase in greenhouse gases in the atmosphere and rising temperatures will increase risk of drought and intensity of storms like tropical cyclones and monsoons.

What the scientific community regards as overwhelming evidence that global warming is a human-made problem and a significant danger to the planet, however, has been disputed by those known as "deniers." Deniers claim, rightly, that climate change events such as the Ice Age have occurred previously. They believe that humankind has overreacted to its potential effects. They politicize the issue in claiming that it is a hoax created to further the agendas of left-wing or scientific organizations.

Many believe that the real threat is not the comparatively small number of people who dismiss the effects of global warming as either nonexistent or exaggerated. Rather, they contend that it is the politicians of the world who seek to cater to those people and the industrial powers that gain from businesses that pollute the environment. Simply stated, curbing the effects of climate change clashes with big business and the economies of industrialized nations.

Among those who have claimed climate change to be a hoax is US president Donald Trump, who, once in office, sought to strip away business regulations limiting carbon emissions and worked to bolster the coal industry in direct conflict with scientific evidence citing its dangers. His stated, but as of yet unproven, belief is that deregulation will result in an employment boom in the coal industry and other businesses. But his detractors have complained that his motivation is simply to line the pockets of corporate America at the expense of the world's environmental health.

A sense of urgency from the United States over climate change was reflected by the policies of the previous administration. President Barack Obama had not only created many initiatives to reduce greenhouse gas emissions and fossil fuel consumption, but he also helped ratify an international agreement in Paris along with seventy-one other countries. The nations of the world that agreed to limit warming by 3.6 degrees Fahrenheit were responsible for nearly 57 percent of all global emissions.

Trump's policies threatened to overturn everything Obama had accomplished in recognizing and combatting the effects of climate change. A 2017 executive order he issued two months after assuming the presidency did not in itself remove American obligation to the Paris accords, but its intent to reinvigorate the coal industry and stop governmental attempts to curb carbon dioxide discharges angered and worried environmentalists and the scientific community as well as millions of his own citizens.

Administration officials sought to calm nerves in their claim that policies could strike a balance between growing the economy, creating jobs, and maintaining environmental responsibility. But when Environmental Protection Agency head Scott Pruitt refuted scientific research by arguing baselessly that carbon dioxide was not the primary contributor to climate change, many worried that Trump was not just more interested in eliminating regulations against corporations, but that he also truly believed global warming was a hoax perpetrated by the Chinese, as he had claimed previously.

Some felt it frightening that world leaders who set policies could have more impact on the future than scientists and others who study climate change for a living. They can only hope that those leaders listen to the urgings of the experts. But if economic concerns override the climate future of the planet, words of wisdom and knowledge will be ignored. And, if it's not too late, future generations would be left to avert disaster.

The viewpoints in this anthology explore the various views on climate change and what effect it might have on our future. The appendixes, "What You Should Know About Our Climate's Future" and "What You Should Do About Our Climate's Future," provide additional information about the issue and give suggestions for taking action. *Issues That Concern You: Our Climate Future* offers a resource for everyone interested in this topic and the future of the globe.

ONE

It's Time to Face the Reality of Climate Change

James Dyke

> In the following viewpoint, James Dyke expresses concern that the actions taken to combat climate change have not kept up with the worsening conditions caused by the problem. He cites record-breaking high temperatures across the globe, including in the Arctic, where he believes the melting of glaciers will have catastrophic results that potentially cannot be reversed. Dyke further states that the momentum of the pace of global warming could eventually be too great to prevent disaster. Dyke is a lecturer in complex systems simulation at the University of Southampton in England.

And another one bites the dust. The year 2014 was the warmest ever recorded by humans. Then 2015 was warmer still. January 2016 broke the record for the largest monthly temperature anomaly. Then came last month.

February didn't break climate change records—it obliterated them. Regions of the Arctic were more than 16°C warmer than normal—whatever constitutes normal now. But what is really making people stand up and notice is that the surface of the Earth north of the equator was 2°C warmer than pre-industrial temperatures. This was meant to be a line that must not be crossed.

Two degrees was broadly interpreted as the temperature that could produce further, potentially runaway warming. You can think of it as a speed limit on our climate impact. But it's not a target speed. If you are driving a car carrying a heavy load down a steep hill you're often advised to change down from top gear and keep your speed low, as if you go too fast your brakes will fail and you will be unable to stop. Less braking means more speed which means less braking—a dangerous runaway feedback loop. Hopefully the hill flattens out and you have enough straight road ahead to recover. If you don't then you will be stopping much more abruptly.

The Reality

We are currently swamping the Earth's ability to absorb greenhouse gases. 2015 saw the largest annual increase in carbon dioxide since records began—far higher than the Earth has experienced for hundreds of thousands of years.

More carbon dioxide in the atmosphere means higher temperatures. There is already one positive feedback loop in operation; the extra warming from our emissions is increasing the amount of water vapour in the atmosphere, which further increases temperatures. Fortunately, this is not a very strong feedback loop.

Unfortunately, there seem to be other, much more powerful ones lurking in the event of further warming. Tipping points such as the thaw of permafrost and release of the very powerful greenhouse gas methane in large quantities would drive world temperatures well beyond the 2°C threshold.

Even if we came to our collective senses and rapidly reduced carbon emissions at that point, we would still have to revert to drastic geoengineering to rein in further warming. There is no guarantee that such climate brakes will work. If they fail, our civilisation would be on a collision course with a much hotter planet.

The safe–unsafe threshold of 2°C recognises the significant amount of uncertainty there is over where dangerous warming really begins. It could be at more than 2°C. Hopefully it is. But it's not impossible that it is less. We need to bear in mind that it

Many scientists believe that melting glaciers in the Arctic caused by progressively warmer global temperatures will have significant—some say catastrophic—effects.

was only the northern hemisphere that crossed the 2°C line. Also, we need to factor in the monster El Niño that is having an effect on temperatures across the globe. In 2014, I predicted that 2015 would break record temperatures. This is not due to any psychic powers on my part, but the then very clear El Niño signal that was emerging.

The Current Landscape

So while temperature records may continue to be set for the rest of 2016, by the end of this year the situation should have cooled somewhat. Right? At times, it feels as if such statements are offered up as prayers in the hope that we are not in fact witnessing the beginning of abrupt and sustained climate change. But what's even scarier is the political, economic and social reaction to these landmarks in climate change.

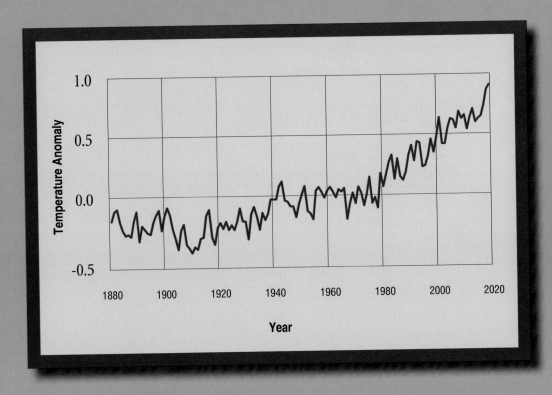

Source: NASA

Have you heard any political speeches referring to these recent climate change records? Not one of the major Republican presidential candidates even "believes" in human-produced climate change, let alone that it is something to worry about.

How was the stock market this morning? It appears febrile enough to lurch from euphoric boom to catastrophic bust on the basis of bland statements from central bankers but proves remarkably deaf to evidence that the entire industrial and financial system is headed for disaster.

Know what's trending on Twitter as I write? A photoshopped giant dog, the latest Game of Thrones trailer and Kim Kardashian's naked body. Actually, it's mainly Kim Kardashian's naked body and people's responses to it. Followed by people's responses to the responses.

It would be churlish of me to deny people the pleasure of looking at pictures of a photograph of a cuddly dog adjusted in order to make it appear both cute and monstrous. But we appear disinterested, either through denial or desensitisation, to the environmental changes happening right in front of our eyes.

There are sure to be more climate records broken this year. But we treat them as we treat new fashions, phones or films. More novelty, newer features, more drama. We seem unable to understand that we are driving such changes. Record breaking changes that will ultimately break our civilisation, and so scatter all that we obsess and care about.

TWO

Climate Change Could Result in an Avalanche of Tsunamis

Christopher Mims

In the following viewpoint, Christopher Mims asserts that the terrible tsunamis that ravaged Japan in recent years should serve as a warning for the rest of the world to take every step possible to curb and reverse climate change. Mims argues that global warming might be a perfect recipe for tsunamis, such as those that killed thousands in Japan, and could do the same along the densely populated shores of the United States and other countries around the world. His contentions lead one to believe that unless world leaders can create policies that stem the tide of rising global temperatures, more killer tsunamis could be on the way. Mims has worked as an editor at *Scientific American*, *Smithsonian*, and *Grist*, and currently is a technology columnist at the *Wall Street Journal*.

So far, today's tsunami has mainly affected Japan—there are reports of up to 300 dead in the coastal city of Sendai—but future tsunamis could strike the U.S. and virtually any other coastal area of the world with equal or greater force, say scientists. In a little-heeded warning issued at a 2009 conference on the subject, experts outlined a range of mechanisms by which climate change could already be causing more earthquakes, tsunamis, and

"Does Climate Change Mean More Tsunamis?" by Christopher Mims, Grist.org, March 12, 2011. Reprinted by permission.

The earthquake and tsunami that hit northeastern Japan in 2011 devastated homes and businesses throughout the area.

volcanic activity, albeit of a scale and nature quite different from Friday's tragedy.

A 2009 paper by Bill McGuire, professor at University College London, says "observations suggest that the ongoing rise in global average temperatures may already be eliciting a hazardous response from the geosphere."

The Product of Catastrophic Events

It's important to note that this response has nothing to do with Friday's tsunami, which is a "subduction zone earthquake," whereas the tsunamis discussed by scientists cited here would be the product of catastrophic events—collapse of methane hydrate deposits at the bottom of the ocean on the continental shelf, for

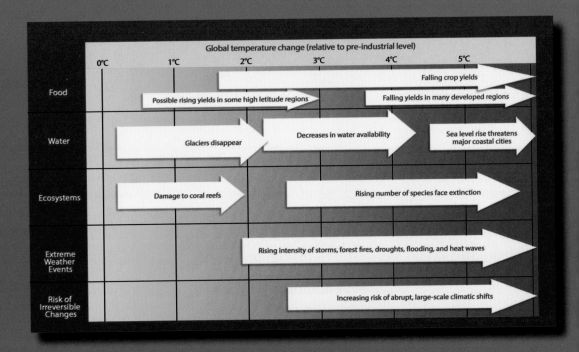

Source: N. Stern

example—for which a tsunami would be but one of many negative impacts.

"When the ice is lost, the earth's crust bounces back up again and that triggers earthquakes, which trigger submarine landslides, which cause tsunamis," McGuire told Reuters. (McGuire's 2009 paper notes that such effects will be much more pronounced in areas with significant ice cover, in other words, at higher latitudes.)

Melting ice masses change the pressures on the underlying earth, which can lead to earthquakes and tsunamis, but that's just the beginning. Rising seas also change the balance of mass across earth's surface, putting new strain on old earthquake faults.

Even a simple change in the weather can dramatically affect the earth beneath our feet:

> David Pyle of Oxford University said small changes in the mass of the earth's surface seems to affect volcanic activity in general, not just in places where ice receded after a cold spell. Weather patterns also seem to affect volcanic activity—not just the other way round, he told the conference.

Scientists have known for some time that climate change affects not just the atmosphere and the oceans but also the earth's crust. These effects are not widely understood by the public.

"In the political community people are almost completely unaware of any geological aspects to climate change," said McGuire.

The Risk Is High

The pace of the response of earth's geosphere to the rapid climate change we are currently experiencing is up for debate. It seems logical that rapid climate change would lead to rapid geological response, as in past eras of climate change as revealed in the fossil record.

Parts of the earth that are now rarely affected by tsunamis, such as northern coastal regions, could be hit by "glacial earthquakes," in which glacier ice crashes to earth in massive landslides.

> "Our experiments show that glacial earthquakes can generate far more powerful tsunamis than undersea earthquakes with similar magnitude," said Song.
>
> "Several high-latitude regions, such as Chile, New Zealand and Canadian Newfoundland are particularly at risk."

Of course, by the time such "glacial earthquakes" were occurring, they would be the least of our worries.

> "Added to all the rest of the mayhem and chaos, these things would just be the icing on the cake," [McGuire] said. "Things would be so bad that the odd tsunami or eruption won't make much difference."

And now for a bit of editorializing: It's often difficult to visualize what climate change-related disasters might look like, but the images pouring out of Japan are visually reminiscent of storm surges supercharged by more powerful weather and rising seas, and of course potential climate change-caused tsunamis. (All of America's coastal cities are vulnerable to these impacts—including ... New York City.) Right on the heels of Brisbane, Snowpocalypse, and Australia's record dust storms, we have yet another reminder of what an Earth transformed by climate change could look like, even though those transformations will play out in ways that are distinct from Friday's tragedy.

THREE

Is There a Connection Between Hurricanes and Global Warming?

Stefan Rahmstorf, Michael Mann, Rasmus Benestad, Gavin Schmidt, and William Connolley

> In the following viewpoint, written in the years following Hurricane Katrina, Stefan Rahmstorf, Michael Mann, Rasmus Benestad, Gavin Schmidt, and William Connolley investigate a potential connection between the hurricane and global warming. Their results were inconclusive, as they claimed that evidence from one meteorological occurrence—albeit a devastating one—could not prove such a connection. However, the authors did contend that statistical evidence points to such a connection. More frankly, the authors urge, the world community must not turn a blind eye to the mounting number of weather-related disasters and dismiss them as being unrelated. The authors are physicists and climate modelers and are permanent contributors to RealClimate.org.

On Monday August 29, Hurricane Katrina ravaged New Orleans, Louisiana and Mississippi, leaving a trail of destruction in her wake. It will be some time until the full toll of this hurricane can be assessed, but the devastating human and environmental impacts are already obvious.

Katrina was the most feared of all meteorological events, a major hurricane making landfall in a highly-populated low-lying

"Hurricanes and Global Warming–Is There a Connection?" by Stefan Rahmstorf, Michael Mann, Rasmus Benestad, Gavin Schmidt, and William Connolley, RealClimate, September 2005. Reprinted by permission.

region. In the wake of this devastation, many have questioned whether global warming may have contributed to this disaster. Could New Orleans be the first major U.S. city ravaged by human-caused climate change?

The correct answer—the one we have indeed provided in previous posts—is that there is no way to prove that Katrina either was, or was not, affected by global warming. For a single event, regardless of how extreme, such attribution is fundamentally impossible. We only have one Earth, and it will follow only one of an infinite number of possible weather sequences. It is impossible to know whether or not this event would have taken place if we had not increased the concentration of greenhouse gases in the atmosphere as much as we have. Weather events will always result from a combination of deterministic factors (including greenhouse gas forcing or slow natural climate cycles) and stochastic factors (pure chance).

Due to this semi-random nature of weather, it is wrong to blame any one event such as Katrina specifically on global warming—and of course it is just as indefensible to blame Katrina on a long-term natural cycle in the climate.

The Question

Yet this is not the right way to frame the question. As we have also pointed out in previous posts, we can indeed draw some important conclusions about the links between hurricane activity and global warming in a statistical sense. The situation is analogous to rolling loaded dice: one could, if one was so inclined, construct a set of dice where sixes occur twice as often as normal. But if you were to roll a six using these dice, you could not blame it specifically on the fact that the dice had been loaded. Half of the sixes would have occurred anyway, even with normal dice. Loading the dice simply doubled the odds. In the same manner, while we cannot draw firm conclusions about one single hurricane, we can draw some conclusions about hurricanes more generally. In particular, the available scientific evidence indicates that it is likely that global warming will make—and possibly already is making—those

While the devastation caused by Hurricane Katrina cannot be blamed directly on climate change, links can be drawn between global warming and hurricane activity.

Climate Change's Effects on Extreme Weather, Ranked by Strength of Scientific Evidence

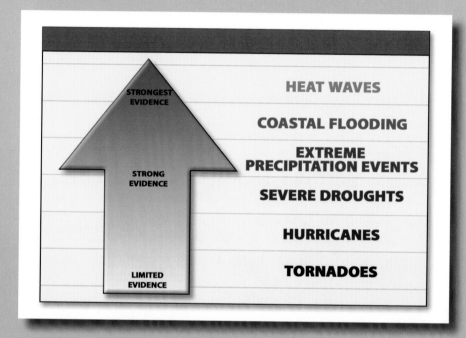

STRONGEST EVIDENCE

STRONG EVIDENCE

LIMITED EVIDENCE

HEAT WAVES

COASTAL FLOODING

EXTREME PRECIPITATION EVENTS

SEVERE DROUGHTS

HURRICANES

TORNADOES

Source: Union of Concerned Scientists

hurricanes that form more destructive than they otherwise would have been.

The key connection is that between sea surface temperatures (we abbreviate this as SST) and the power of hurricanes. Without going into technical details about the dynamics and thermodynamics involved in tropical storms and hurricanes, the basic connection between the two is actually fairly simple: warm water, and the instability in the lower atmosphere that is created by it, is the energy source of hurricanes. This is why they only arise in the tropics and during the season when SSTs are highest (June to November in the tropical North Atlantic).

SST is not the only influence on hurricane formation. Strong shear in atmospheric winds (that is, changes in wind strength and direction with height in the atmosphere above the surface), for example, inhibits development of the highly organized structure that is required for a hurricane to form. In the case of Atlantic hurricanes, the El Nino/Southern Oscillation tends to influence the vertical wind shear, and thus, in turn, the number of hurricanes that tend to form in a given year. Many other features of the process of hurricane development and strengthening, however, are closely linked to SST.

Hurricane forecast models (the same ones that were used to predict Katrina's path) indicate a tendency for more intense (but not overall more frequent) hurricanes when they are run for climate change scenarios.

In one model simulation of hurricane trends, the frequency of the strongest (category 5) hurricanes roughly triples in the anthropogenic climate change scenario relative to the control. This suggests that hurricanes may indeed become more destructive as tropical SSTs warm due to anthropogenic impacts.

Global Warming or Natural Cycle?

But what about the past? What do the observations of the last century actually show? Some past studies (e.g. Goldenberg et al, 2001) assert that there is no evidence of any long-term increase in statistical measures of tropical Atlantic hurricane activity, despite the ongoing global warming. These studies, however, have focused on the frequency of all tropical storms and hurricanes (lumping the weak ones in with the strong ones) rather than a measure of changes in the intensity of the storms. As we have discussed elsewhere on this site, statistical measures that focus on trends in the strongest category storms, maximum hurricane winds, and changes in minimum central pressures, suggest a systematic increase in the intensities of those storms that form. This finding is consistent with the model simulations.

A recent study in *Nature* by Emanuel (2005) examined, for the first time, a statistical measure of the power dissipation associated with past hurricane activity (i.e., the "Power Dissipation Index" or "PDI"). Emanuel found a close correlation between increases in this measure of hurricane activity (which is likely a better measure of the destructive potential of the storms than previously used measures) and rising tropical North Atlantic SST, consistent with basic theoretical expectations. As tropical SSTs have increased in past decades, so has the intrinsic destructive potential of hurricanes.

The key question then becomes this: Why has SST increased in the tropics? Is this increase due to global warming (which is almost certainly in large part due to human impacts on climate)? Or is this increase part of a natural cycle?

It has been asserted (for example, by the NOAA National Hurricane Center) that the recent upturn in hurricane activity is due to a natural cycle, e.g. the so-called Atlantic Multidecadal Oscillation ("AMO"). The new results by Emanuel argue against this hypothesis being the sole explanation: the recent increase in SST (at least for September) is well outside the range of any past oscillations. Emanuel therefore concludes in his paper that "the large upswing in the last decade is unprecedented, and probably reflects the effect of global warming." However, caution is always warranted with very new scientific results until they have been thoroughly discussed by the community and either supported or challenged by further analyses. Previous analysis of the AMO and natural oscillation modes in the Atlantic (Delworth and Mann, 2000; Kerr, 2000) suggest that the amplitude of natural SST variations averaged over the tropics is about 0.1–0.2 °C, so a swing from the coldest to warmest phase could explain up to ~0.4 °C warming.

What about the alternative hypothesis: the contribution of anthropogenic greenhouse gases to tropical SST warming? How strong do we expect this to be? One way to estimate this is to use climate models. Driven by anthropogenic forcings, these show a warming of tropical SST in the Atlantic of about 0.2–0.5 °C. Globally, SST has increased by ~0.6 °C in the past hundred years. This mostly reflects the response to global radiative forcings, which are dominated by anthropogenic forcing over the 20th Century. Regional modes of variability, such as the AMO, largely cancel out and make a very small contribution in the global mean SST changes.

Conclusions

Thus, we can conclude that both a natural cycle (the AMO) and anthropogenic forcing could have made roughly equally large contributions to the warming of the tropical Atlantic over the past decades, with an exact attribution impossible so far. The observed warming is likely the result of a combined effect: data strongly suggest that the AMO has been in a warming phase for the past two or three decades, and we also know that at the same time anthropogenic global warming is ongoing.

Finally, then, we come back to Katrina. This storm was a weak (category 1) hurricane when crossing Florida, and only gained force later over the warm waters of the Gulf of Mexico. So the question to ask here is: why is the Gulf of Mexico so hot at present—how much of this could be attributed to global warming, and how much to natural variability? More detailed analysis of the SST changes in the relevant regions, and comparisons with model predictions, will probably shed more light on this question in the future. At present, however, the available scientific evidence suggests that it would be premature to assert that the recent anomalous behavior can be attributed entirely to a natural cycle.

But ultimately the answer to what caused Katrina is of little practical value. Katrina is in the past. Far more important is learning something for the future, as this could help reduce the risk of further tragedies. Better protection against hurricanes will be an obvious discussion point over the coming months, to which as climatologists we are not particularly qualified to contribute. But climate science can help us understand how human actions influence climate. The current evidence strongly suggests that:

(a) hurricanes tend to become more destructive as ocean temperatures rise, and

(b) an unchecked rise in greenhouse gas concentrations will very likely increase ocean temperatures further, ultimately overwhelming any natural oscillations.

Scenarios for future global warming show tropical SST rising by a few degrees, not just tenths of a degree. That is the important message from science. What we need to discuss is not what caused Katrina, but the likelihood that global warming will make hurricanes even worse in future.

References

Delworth, T.L., Mann, M.E., Observed and Simulated Multidecadal Variability in the Northern Hemisphere, *Climate Dynamics*, 16, 661-676, 2000.

Emanuel, K. (2005), Increasing destructiveness of tropical cyclones over the past 30 years, *Nature*, online publication; published online 31 July 2005 | doi: 10.1038/nature03906

Goldenberg, S.B., C.W. Landsea, A.M. Mestas-Nuñez, and W.M. Gray. The recent increase in Atlantic hurricane activity. Causes and implications. *Science*, 293:474-479 (2001).

Kerr, R.A., 2000, A North Atlantic climate pacemaker for the centuries: *Science*, v. 288, p. 1984-1986.

Knutson, T. K., and R. E. Tuleya, 2004: Impact of CO_2-induced warming on simulated hurricane intensity and precipitation: Sensitivity to the choice of climate model and convective parameterization. *Journal of Climate*, 17(18), 3477-3495.

FOUR

The Importance of the Paris Agreement

Center for Climate and Energy Solutions

In the following excerpted viewpoint, the Center for Climate and Energy Solutions unpacks the Paris Agreement and its potential effects on the battle against climate change. The Paris Agreement resulted from the 21st Conference of the Parties (COP) of the UNFCCC in 2015. Included among the important provisions of the agreement signed by the major polluters of the world, and since rejected by the United States, was a commitment to reduce carbon emissions that have threatened the ozone layer and played a huge role in creating global warming. The Center for Climate and Energy Solutions is a nonpartisan, independent organization seeking practical solutions to global warming and its effects.

The Paris Agreement

In broad structure, the Paris Agreement reflects a "hybrid" approach blending bottom-up flexibility, to achieve broad participation, with top-down rules, to promote accountability and ambition.

Legal Character

The Paris Agreement is a treaty under international law, but only certain provisions are legally binding.

The issue of which provisions to make binding (expressed as "shall," as opposed to "should") was a central concern for many

"Outcomes of the U.N. Climate Change Conference in Paris," by the Center for Climate and Energy Solutions, November 30–December 12, 2015. Reprinted with permission of the Center for Climate and Energy Solutions.

countries, in particular the United States, which wanted an agreement the president could accept without seeking congressional approval. Meeting that test precluded binding emission targets and new binding financial commitments.

A final step in Paris was negotiating a "technical correction" substituting "should" for "shall" in a provision calling on developed countries to undertake absolute economy-wide emissions targets.

Differentiation

A crosscutting issue was how to reflect the UNFCCC's principle of "common but differentiated responsibilities and respective capabilities." On the whole, the Paris Agreement represents a fundamental shift away from the categorical binary approach of the Kyoto Protocol toward more nuanced forms of differentiation, reflected differently in different provisions.

The agreement includes references to developed and developing countries, stating in several places that the former should take the lead. But it notably makes no mention of the Annex I (developed) and non-Annex I (developing) categories contained in the UNFCCC.

Many provisions establish common commitments while allowing flexibility to accommodate different national capacities and circumstances—either through self-differentiation, as implicit in the concept of nationally determined contributions, or through more detailed operational rules still to be developed.

Long-Term Goal

The agreement reaffirms the goal of keeping average warming below 2 degrees Celsius, while also urging parties to "pursue efforts" to limit it to 1.5 degrees, a top priority for developing countries highly vulnerable to climate impacts.

Mitigation

The Paris Agreement articulates two long-term emission goals: first, a peaking of emissions as soon as possible (with a recognition

Nations Unies
Conférence sur les Changements Climatiques 2015

COP21/CMP11

Paris, France

World leaders convened in Paris, France, in late 2015 for a two-week United Nations climate change summit.

that it will take longer for developing countries); then, a goal of net greenhouse gas neutrality (expressed as "a balance between anthropogenic emissions by sources and removals by sinks") in the second half of this century. The latter was an alternative to terms like "decarbonization" and "climate neutrality" pushed by some parties.

With respect to countries' individual mitigation efforts, the agreement prescribes a set of binding procedural commitments: to "prepare, communicate and maintain" a nationally determined conribution (NDC); to provide information necessary for clarity and transparency; and to communicate a new NDC every five years. It also sets the expectation that each successive NDC will "represent a progression" beyond the previous one and reflect a party's "highest possible ambition."

The agreement commits parties to "pursue domestic measures with the aim of achieving the objectives" of its NDC, but does not make the implementation or achievement of NDCs a binding obligation. It also encourages, but does not require, countries to develop and communicate long-term low emission development strategies.

The core mitigation commitments are common to all parties, but there is some differentiation in the expectations set: developed countries "should" undertake absolute economy-wide reduction targets, while developing countries "are encouraged" to move toward economy-wide targets over time. In addition, developing countries are to receive support to implement their commitments.

NDCs will be recorded in a public registry maintained by the UNFCCC secretariat, rather than in an annex to the agreement, as some countries had proposed.

Carbon Markets

While avoiding any direct reference to the use of market-based approaches—a concession to a handful of countries that oppose them—the agreement recognizes that parties may use "internationally transferred mitigation outcomes" to implement their NDCs.

It requires that parties engaging in such transfers ensure the "avoidance of double counting," consistent with accounting guidelines for NDCs to be developed. The agreement also establishes a new mechanism to succeed the Kyoto Protocol's Clean Development Mechanism, which generates tradable emission offsets. Rules for the new mechanism are to be adopted at the first meeting of parties after the agreement takes force.

Stockade/Successive NDCs

To promote rising ambition, the agreement establishes two linked processes, each on a five-year cycle.

The first process is a "global stocktake" to assess collective progress toward meeting the agreement's long-term goals. The

Share of Total Global Carbon Dioxide Emissions from Energy Consumption, by Country

China	27%
US	17%
Russia, India	5%
Japan	4%
Germany, Iran, South Korea, Canada, Saudi Arabia, United Kingdom	2%
Brazil, Mexico, South Africa, Italy, Indonesia, Australia, France, Poland, Spain	1%
Rest of World	20%

Source: Union of Concerned Scientists

first stocktake will take place in 2023. The second process is the submission by parties of new NDCs, "informed by the outcomes of the global stocktake."

Because these processes technically begin only once the agreement takes force, the accompanying decision includes provisions to effectively jumpstart them in the interim. It establishes a "facilitative dialogue" in 2018 to take stock of collective progress. And, by 2020, countries like the United States whose initial NDCs run through 2025 are "urged" to communicate "new" NDCs, while those whose initial NDCs run through 2030 are "requested" to "communicate or update" theirs.

Transparency

The Paris Agreement rests heavily on transparency as a means of holding countries accountable. In another move beyond bifurcation, it establishes a new transparency system with common binding commitments for all parties and "built-in flexibility" to accommodate varying national capacities.

All countries are required to submit emissions inventories and the "information necessary to track progress made in implementing and achieving" their NDCs. The COP decision says that, with the exception of least developed and small island countries, these reports are to be submitted at least every two years. In addition, developed countries "shall" report on support provided; developing countries "should" report on support received; and all "should" report on their adaptation efforts.

Information reported by countries on mitigation and support will undergo "expert technical review," and each party must participate in "a facilitative, multilateral consideration of progress" in implementing and achieving its NDC (a form of peer review).

Developing countries are promised capacity-building support to help them meet the new transparency requirements. The COP decision says they will be given flexibility in the scope, frequency and detail of their reporting, and in the scope of review. Details of the new transparency system are to be negotiated by 2018 and formally adopted once the agreement enters into force.

Implementation/Compliance

The agreement establishes a new mechanism to "facilitate implementation" and "promote compliance." The mechanism—a committee of experts—is to be "facilitative" in nature and operate in a "non-adversarial and non-punitive" manner. It will report annually to the COP. Details are to be decided at the first meeting of parties after the agreement takes force.

Finance

As at past COPs, finance was a contentious issue in Paris, with poorer developing countries seeking stronger assurances that support will be scaled up, and developed countries pushing for wealthier developing countries to contribute as well.

Both succeeded to some degree. The agreement commits developed countries to provide finance for mitigation and adaptation in developing countries ("in continuation of their existing obligations under the Convention," a stipulation sought by the United States so the agreement would not create new binding financial commitments requiring congressional approval). "Other" parties are "encouraged" to provide such support "voluntarily."

Other major issues included whether to set a new finance mobilization goal beyond the $100 billion a year in public and private resources already promised by developed countries, and whether to establish a process to revisit the question every five years. The COP decision extends the $100 billion-a-year goal through 2025, and beyond that, says only that by 2025 the COP will set a "new collective quantified goal from a floor of" $100 billion a year.

In addition to reporting on finance already provided and received, developed countries commit to submit every two years "indicative quantitative and qualitative information" on future support, including, "as available," projected levels of public finance; and other countries are encouraged to do so voluntarily. Finance will also be considered in the global stocktake.

Adaptation

A major priority for many developing countries was strengthening adaptation efforts under the UNFCCC. The agreement does that by:

- Establishing a global goal of "enhancing adaptive capacity, strengthening resilience and reducing vulnerability to climate change;"

- Requiring all parties, "as appropriate," to plan and implement adaptation efforts;

- Encouraging all parties to report on their adaptation efforts and/or needs;

- Committing enhanced adaptation support for developing countries; and

- Including a review of adaptation progress, and of the adequacy and effectiveness of adaptation support, in the global stocktake to be undertaken every five years.

Loss and Damage

In a victory for small island countries and other countries highly vulnerable to climate impacts, the agreement includes a free-standing provision extending the Warsaw International Mechanism for Loss and Damage.

The mechanism, established as an interim body at COP 19, is charged with developing approaches to help vulnerable countries cope with unavoidable impacts, including extreme weather events and slow-onset events such as sea-level rise. Potential approaches include early warning systems and risk insurance.

At the insistence of developed countries, led by the United States, the accompanying COP decision specifies that the loss and damage provision "does not involve or provide a basis for any liability or compensation."

FIVE

Are We Doing Enough to Adapt to Climate Change?

David Thompson

In the following viewpoint, David Thompson considers the effects of the 2015 European Climate Change Adaption conference in Denmark. He concludes that progress indeed had been made, but judging that level of progress is far more difficult than measuring more tangible evidence, such as the lowering of greenhouse gas emissions into the environment. The overall tone of the piece is one of optimism but also includes an admission that much more needs to be accomplished. A former senior policy analyst at the Committee on Climate Change, Thompson is senior policy advisor, UK Department of Environment, Food, and Rural Affairs.

Unlike measuring a country's greenhouse gas emissions, which is technically challenging but entirely possible, measuring progress on adaptation is much less clear cut. Nonetheless, in the UK this is a task that falls to the Committee on Climate Change, and in recent years we've made some real strides forward.

Still, it's not easy. Even before we can measure anything, there are a number of obstacles to overcome. First is the degree of uncertainty about the future climate—we do not know exactly how much warmer, wetter, drier or stormier specific parts of the UK might get in the years ahead.

"Are We Doing Enough to Adapt to Climate Change?" by David Thompson, Committee on Climate Change, May 22, 2015. Reprinted by permission.

Advances in technology, such as features in smart homes, have the potential to reduce our carbon footprint.

What we do have are a range of climate projections. At one extreme they suggest parts of the country could experience major climatic changes in the long-term that would require major upheavals, for example relocating towns or investing in new infrastructure. At the other extreme, other projections suggest that the impacts may not be anywhere near as significant. Accounting for changes in population, demographics, technology, global trade and other socio-economic factors add further uncertainty to understanding the size of risks in the future.

So we have no real way of knowing precisely how much we need to adapt, how much it will cost, or by when we need to do it. This makes it inherently difficult to assess how much change is necessary now and what progress is being made towards it.

Where to Start?

Historic greenhouse gas emissions have already "locked-in" a certain amount of climate change, and even if we successfully limit the global temperature rise to no more than 2°C, the world can still expect to see significant impacts.

At a global level, one approach is to simply count the number of adaptation plans and strategies in place. One study presented at the ECCA conference identified over 4,000 discrete adaptation plans and initiatives across 117 countries. In Europe, 21 out of 33 countries have produced national adaptation plans or strategies, including the UK which set out its plan in 2013.

It's also possible to assess whether key organisations in a country have adaptation plans, or are at least thinking about long-term climate change risks. In the UK, almost all infrastructure providers and utility companies produced adaptation plans in 2010-2011 and many are publishing updates in 2015. Local authorities are the other key players. A survey of 90 local councils in England carried out by the Committee on Climate Change this year found that around half have a specific adaptation plan and most are considering the impacts of climate change over the long-term in areas like land-use planning, public health and flood risk management.

Measuring progress in this way is informative, but has its limitations. It is easy to write a plan, or to name-check adaptation in existing plans, but there is often no way of knowing whether those plans are being implemented or whether they are effective in reducing vulnerability on the ground.

Status of State and Local Climate Adaptation Plans, 2017

Source: Georgetown Climate Center

Indicators

That's why the Committee has gone one step further. As part of our upcoming assessment of the UK's progress on adapting to climate change, due out at the end of June, we're also assessing outcomes with indicators. The indicators are designed to tell us what is actually happening to vulnerability to climate change impacts on the ground.

In this way we're able to make a robust and balanced assessment as to whether progress is being made to reduce the UK's vulnerability. For example, is new development appropriately designed to be resilient to flooding, include measures to soak up excess rainwater and water-efficient? If so, then we are likely to be making progress to reduce, or at least not increase, vulnerability to the risks of more severe flooding and drought in the future.

On the other hand, if we find that inappropriate development is going ahead in areas of high flood risk, and that we are paving-over front gardens with hard surfacing, and that new homes are not routinely fitted with water meters, then the UK is almost certainly increasing its vulnerability to climate risks.

To support this analysis the Committee has built up and tested a set of unique indicators across a wide range of themes including the built environment, infrastructure, health, business and the natural environment. This means there is enough evidence to come up with an evaluation of where progress is being made, and where more action is required.

It's not entirely quantitative, as it only gives an indication of progress where data is available and relies on expert judgment, but it's about as robust as it can be given the wide range of uncertainties we face. And based on the reception we received in Copenhagen last week, when it comes to measuring adaptation, it's pretty clear the UK is ahead of the curve.

SIX

The United States Is Backing Away from Climate Change Initiatives

Natasha Geiling

> In the following viewpoint, Natasha Geiling argues that, even before President Donald Trump pulled the United States out of the Paris Agreement, he was already sending the nation's environmental policies tumbling backward through a spate of executive orders. The author asserts that Trump's repeal of the Clean Power Plan, which was put in place by his predecessor, Barack Obama, was merely the first of many orders made by the president that show his disregard or ignorance of the effects of climate change. Geiling writes about climate and the environment for ThinkProgress.

Three months into President Donald Trump's first term, one thing has become increasingly clear: Trump has no interest in maintaining the environmental protections ushered in by President Barack Obama.

Trump looks to solidify that intention on Tuesday, releasing a sweeping executive order that touches nearly every environmental action taken by the previous administration.

"There are a number of policies from the Obama administration that the president believes should be reviewed," a senior

"Trump Just Gutted U.S. Policies to Fight Climate Change," by Natasha Geiling, ThinkProgress, March 28, 2017. Reprinted by permission.

"Nah, climate change isn't real."

This political cartoon pokes fun at those known as climate change deniers, who may come around too late to reverse the effects global warming has had on the earth.

White House official said during a press call on Monday night. "Some of them should be taken off the books immediately, to the extent that we can."

In the order, the president asks for more than just a repeal and rework of the Clean Power Plan, Obama's signature domestic climate policy and Trump's preferred scapegoat for the declining coal industry. The order also seeks to repeal rules regarding fracking on public lands, and coal leases on federal lands. It orders agencies to reconsider the Social Cost of Carbon and rescinds an Obama-era order requiring agencies to consider the impact of climate change in their environmental permitting process. And it undoes key executive actions meant to make the federal government—and communities—more prepared to handle the consequences of climate change.

Reports have been circulating for months regarding this order and its contents, but the timeline for its release slipped more than once. As the weeks stretched on, the executive order became about more than just the Clean Power Plan—the Trump administration, acting not unlike a five-year-old left unsupervised in the aisles of a candy store, kept piling on rules and regulations it wanted to include.

The result is a behemoth order that touches on nearly a dozen different Obama-era rules. And while it will certainly have a measurable impact on domestic energy policy for years to come, the order—like Trump's proposed "skinny budget" released in mid-March—is also a values statement, one that signals the United States federal government is no longer interested in fighting climate change, or helping communities adapt to its devastating consequences, at home and abroad.

This Order Will Make Communities More Vulnerable to Climate Change

While the order is being touted as a job creator by the Trump White House, it's important to note that it sends a clear signal to agencies across the federal government: climate change is no longer something that should be considered a priority when making decisions.

That's evident in the order's directive to repeal a number of Obama-era executive actions aimed at mitigating impacts on natural resources from development, requiring federal agencies to take steps to prepare for climate impacts, and requiring agencies to take climate change into account when crafting national security plans and policies.

The Trump executive order also unilaterally rescinds President Obama's Climate Action Plan, which served as the blueprint for climate action under the previous administration.

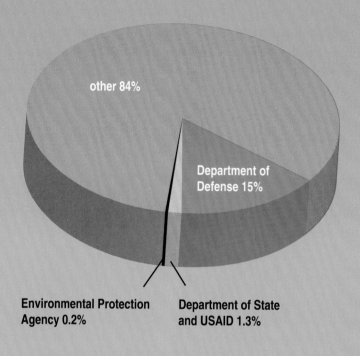

Distribution of Total Federal Spending, 2016

other 84%

Department of
Defense 15%

Environmental Protection
Agency 0.2%

Department of State
and USAID 1.3%

Source: Office of Management and Budget

"We believe a number of those orders have run their course, we also believe those orders simply don't reflect the president's priorities when it comes to dealing with climate change," a senior White House official said on Monday.

Trump does not accept the scientific consensus on climate change, and has claimed it is a hoax created by the Chinese to make the U.S. less competitive in manufacturing. His EPA head, Scott Pruitt, also does not accept the scientific consensus on climate change, falsely claiming carbon dioxide emissions are not a primary contributor to global warming.

In fact, 97 percent of scientists agree that climate change is both real and a result of human activity.

Government agencies may choose to continue to consider climate change in their planning processes, even after Obama's executive orders are repealed. The Department of Defense, for instance, has long sounded alarm bells about the danger climate change poses to both national security and U.S. operations abroad. It's unlikely they will stop taking climate impacts into account, especially with Secretary of Defense James Mattis citing climate change as a threat to American interests at home and abroad in unpublished testimony provided to the Senate Armed Services Committee after his confirmation hearing. Other agencies, however, may stop factoring climate change into their policy-making process since they are no longer required to do so.

This Order Won't Bring Back the Jobs Trump Promises It Will

On the campaign trail, Trump touted an energy platform that was heavy on promises and light on policy. He promised to bring back coal jobs and revitalize the shrinking industry, whose decline he blamed on Obama-era regulations like the Clean Power Plan. He also promised to unleash American natural gas extraction, pledging to open up drilling on federal lands and in previously off-limits coastal areas.

"We're going to bring back jobs," Vice President Mike Pence said before a crowd in West Virginia on Saturday. "We're going to get Washington out of the way of energy producers and coal miners—because energy means growth for America, and President Trump digs coal."

Energy experts and economists, however, have been quick to point out that it might be near impossible for Trump to deliver on his promises, especially in coal country. For starters, Trump's promises to coal country and the natural gas industry are at odds with one another: If he succeeds in encouraging natural gas production, the low cost and wide availability of natural gas will likely only deepen coal's decline. And reworking the Clean Power Plan, according to the Energy Information Administration, will do little to help hasten coal's rebound—coal was suffering long before the

Clean Power Plan, due to both automation in the coal industry and the cheap, plentiful natural gas. (The Clean Power Plan, incidentally, hasn't even been implemented because it's under a stay from the U.S. Supreme Court.)

"I think it's mostly symbolic gesture by the administration," John Coequyt, Sierra Club's senior campaign director for federal and international climate campaigns, told ThinkProgress. "It's the Trump administration saying we don't believe that climate change is a problem that needs to be addressed, and trying, I believe, to align itself with the communities that have been struggling with this transition without actually addressing the problems of those communities."

Lifting the moratorium on new coal leases on federal lands is also unlikely to do much to bring back coal jobs in the near-term. Forty percent of U.S. coal comes from federal lands, mainly from the Powder River Basin in Wyoming and Montana, but the federal government hasn't sold a new coal lease on federal lands since 2012. Competition from cheap natural gas and renewable energy has thrown coal's long-term economic viability into question, and many coal companies already have federal leases that span five, 10, or 20 years into the future—meaning even without the moratorium, demand for those leases is unlikely to be high enough to radically alter slumping demand for coal. Peabody, the country's largest coal company, for instance, told Bloomberg that it would not need another federal coal lease for "approximately a decade at this point."

Despite EPA Administrator Scott Pruitt's assertion on ABC's *This Week* that the executive order would "absolutely" bring back coal jobs, it's unlikely coal communities will see immediate relief from this new executive order. The order does not address the issue of automation in the coal industry, which has been responsible for rapid reductions in mining employment. It also does nothing to combat the competition coal faces from cheap natural gas—if fact, Trump has regularly expressed support for expanded fracking in the United States, a policy that would further deepen coal's decline.

The order also does nothing to provide health care to tens of thousands of retired coal miners, who are facing the expiration of health care benefits in April. It also does nothing to soften cuts to regional programs proposed in the Trump "skinny budget," including zeroing out the Appalachian Regional Commission, a program that helps fund everything from infrastructure updates to job training programs in communities hit hardest by coal's downturn.

Moreover, repealing the Clean Power Plan—coupled with cuts to renewable energy and energy efficiency funding proposed in Trump's budget—could hurt a sector of the economy that has been experiencing rapid growth in recent years: renewable energy. According to a report from the Environmental Defense Fund, wind and solar have been adding jobs at a rate 12 times as fast as the rest of the economy, and the Bureau of Labor Statistics expects that the fastest growing job over the next decade will likely be a wind turbine technician.

This Order Won't Increase America's Energy Independence

Pruitt, Trump, and White House Press Secretary Sean Spicer have all touted Tuesday's order as a move to reduce the country's dependence on foreign energy sources and increase energy independence—but it's far from a sure thing that the order will actually accomplish this.

Eliminating the Clean Power Plan (a process this order merely sets into motion) likely wouldn't have a significant impact on the country's energy imports. If anything, it would shift America's energy mix to slightly favor coal, away from lower-carbon alternatives like renewable energy.

Lifting the coal moratorium is also likely to have a negligible impact—at least in the near term—on U.S. energy independence, as many coal companies currently have sufficient reserves to meet demand. Similarly, lifting rules for fracking on public lands is unlikely to substantially boost production in those areas; the Obama-era rules did not prevent fracking, but simply required stronger environmental standards and reporting from companies that drill on public lands. According to analysis from the Department of the Interior, those rules would have increased the cost of production per well by less than a quarter of one percent — probably not a large enough margin to seriously impact production.

Doing away with the Obama-era rule meant to limit methane from oil and gas operations will likely result in more wasted methane from those operations—increasing waste in the U.S. energy sector, not spurring production. An economic analysis from the Environmental Defense Fund found that scrapping the rule could result in loses of natural gas worth up to $330 million each year.

This Order Means Years of Legal Battles Are Ahead

Many of the marquee regulations the Trump administration is seeking to repeal with this order—the Clean Power Plan, limits on methane from existing oil and gas operations, standards for fracking on public lands—cannot be unilaterally repealed with the stroke of the pen. Other parts of this order—the portion targeting the Social Cost of Carbon, for instance, or the elimination of the Council on Environment Quality's National Environmental Policy Act guidance on climate change—can be accomplished with the stroke of the pen, but definitely open the administration up to legal challenges in the future.

The bottom line is that Trump, like all presidents, has to operate within the bounds of what he can and can't do by executive order. With this sprawling order, he's certainly tried his hardest to do as much as he can, unilaterally, to reverse the Obama administration's climate progress.

But there are still hurdles the Trump administration must clear in order to fully undo final rules; the Clean Power Plan, for instance, will need to go through a rule-making process, which includes periods for public comment, before a new rule can be finalized. It will also need to defend any changes to the rule, a task potentially made much more difficult in light of Trump's many public statements about his intent to kill the Clean Power Plan, words that could come back to haunt a Trump administration defending changes to the plan as neither arbitrary nor politically motivated. In a call with reporters on Monday night, a senior White House official acknowledged that the rewriting of the Clean Power Plan would likely face legal challenges in court, and that the final rule would "likely take some time."

Environmental legal experts agree with that analysis.

"Each of these rollbacks face many obstacles," David Doniger, senior attorney for Natural Resources Defense Council's climate and clean air program, said on a press call in advance of the order. "The orders we may see don't change the rules on the books, and tearing those rules down requires going through the same steps as it took to build them up."

In rolling back Obama-era regulations or rules, the Trump administration will also have to contend with years of established environmental law. A 2007 Supreme Court ruling found that the EPA has authority, under the Clean Air Act, to regulate carbon dioxide—if the EPA chooses to renege on that authority, it's likely that the agency will be challenged in court. The same goes for using the Social Cost of Carbon in decision-making: a different 2007 court order directed the George W. Bush administration to consider the value of cutting carbon pollution in creating vehicle fuel economy standards, and it's likely environmental groups would challenge future decisions that do not take the value of cutting carbon dioxide into account.

And while it's unclear exactly how those challenges will play out in court, one thing appears certain: environmental groups are ready to fight.

"This is the starting gun," Sierra Club's Coequty said of the order. "It initiates a very long fight."

SEVEN

The New President Is Foiling a Clean Energy Economy

Ryan Koronowski

> In the following viewpoint, Ryan Koronowski uses the fears about then-presidential candidate Donald Trump's stance on climate change and the environment to highlight how far we've come in environmental reform—and how easily we could regress. Koronowski was bracing for the worst after Trump had already indicated his desire to invigorate the dying coal industry and called climate change a hoax perpetrated by China. Koronowski turned out to be a bit of a prophet in his prediction that Trump would be an enemy of environmentalists and those who seek to reverse the effects of climate change. Koronowski is research director at ThinkProgress.

If Donald Trump becomes the next president of the United States, well, many things will happen. The stock market could crash. U.S. allies could have to reimagine their relationships with America. The population of Canada would get a bump.

He will also have to decide what he would actually do with U.S. energy and climate policy. He's already offered some rhetoric about saving coal jobs, denying climate science, and bashing renewable energy. But on Thursday he is expected to reveal his agenda in keynote speech at an oil expo in Bismarck, North Dakota.

"The Environmental Implications of a Trump Presidency," by Ryan Koronowski, ThinkProgress, May 27, 2016. Reprinted by permission.

"I have no idea what Trump thinks about climate change," said Alex Bozmoski, strategy and policy director at the conservative environmental group RepublicEn. "Donald Trump as the standard-bearer for the Republican Party is a pontificator's paradise because there's no connection between what he says and what he does."

For the most part, Trump's views have been predominantly expressed on Twitter—largely about how cold weather in the winter meant mainstream climate science was a joke, and how much he disliked wind turbines.

"Building a clean energy economy takes more than 140 characters," Tom Steyer, president of NextGen Climate said on a Wednesday press call. Trump isn't alone in this effort to foil a clean energy economy, he said—he leads a party that has embraced polluters, tried to block the EPA's anti-pollution efforts.

Rep. Kevin Cramer (R-ND) was recently announced as Trump's energy advisor. Cramer likes fossil fuel extraction, dislikes environmental regulations, and says mainstream climate science is based on "fraudulent science." Trump's speech to the oil industry in North Dakota may provide further clarity.

But what would a President Trump's real-world options be when it comes to changing current energy and climate policy?

Stopping Environmental Executive Action

The Obama Administration has one main option in response to a GOP-controlled legislative body that is by nearly all accounts the most anti-environment congress in history. It can enforce current laws on the books in new ways, issuing rules and executive orders to cut pollution and boost sustainable solutions around the government and nation. These have been successful in many ways.

This is also the easiest way for a new president to reverse Obama's progress on the environment.

Brad Johnson, executive director of Climate Hawks Vote, said that Trump is not a conventional candidate. "He says he would bomb countries and take their oil. That's what he would do. He says that global warming is a Chinese hoax—he would treat scientists and environmentalists as threats to the state."

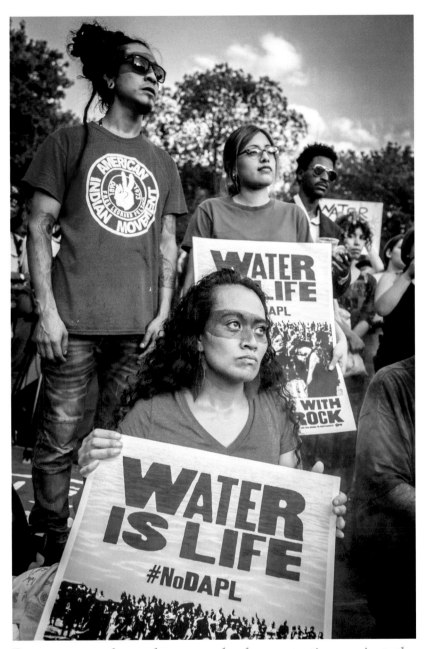

Protesters, such as these people demonstrating against the Dakota Access Pipeline, stand up to the US government on behalf of the environment.

Johnson said Trump "would take extreme executive action," easily dismantling Obama's executive actions.

Energy Secretary Ernest Moniz said, however, that it would be difficult for the next president to undo all the formal rulemaking, especially as the markets and industry have already begun to adjust to cleaner energy.

Scrapping the EPA, Let Alone the Clean Power Plan

When a presidential candidate says they will eliminate the EPA, calling it a "disgrace," a serious consideration of his environmental policy gets a little screwy.

"Trump has said explicitly that he wants to eliminate the EPA so there is no speculation on how far he would try to go," Holly Shulman, a Sierra Club spokesperson, told ThinkProgress. Most Americans across the political spectrum support the EPA's safeguards, she said, and coal is on its way out. "Donald Trump can talk about eliminating the EPA until his face turns blue but the market won't support it," Shulman said.

What of President Obama's signature climate policy, the Clean Power Plan? Trump could potentially slow down or stop the rule, which regulates carbon pollution from the power sector through a flexible arrangement with each state. It's currently being fought in court, with oral arguments scheduled for September 27.

Rhea Suh, president of the NRDC Action Fund, said on a Wednesday press call that Trump could have EPA withdraw the Clean Power Plan altogether, he could fight it in court, and he could assure the states that their plans would not be enforced strongly, if at all. Suh noted that delaying regulations like methane standards and clean vehicle standards "would be in essence a defeat" given how quickly emissions need to drop.

Trump responded in an American Energy Alliance (AEA) questionnaire that he would review the EPA's "endangerment finding" which undergirds the premise that greenhouse gases are able to be regulated under the Clean Air Act if they endager public health and welfare. The Supreme Court said the Bush

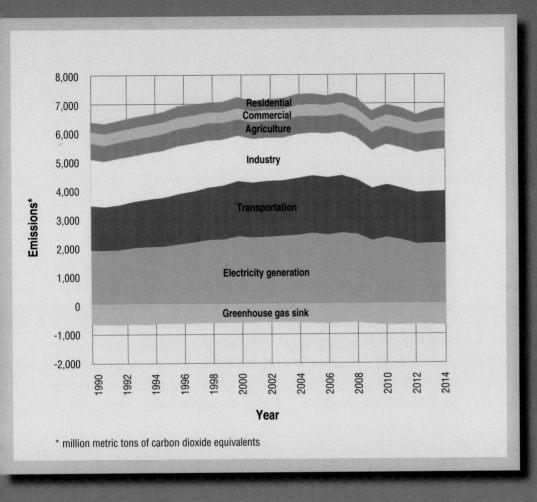

Year

* million metric tons of carbon dioxide equivalents

Source: EPA

administration had to regulate carbon dioxide under the Act if the EPA found such a threat. In 2009, it did exactly that, and from there the administration has regulated carbon pollution from vehicles and the power sector to comply with the law. Reviewing the endangerment finding could threaten that work.

RepublicEn's Bozmoski was skeptical of this move. "If he doesn't have the votes to shut down the EPA, perhaps he could use a stunt like that to get everyone to quit," he told ThinkProgress. "It feels sinister to instruct civil servants and scientists to anchor the policy of the U.S. to wildly-discredited, un-empirical junk science."

If Trump can't shut down the EPA, he will still do his best to stop it from doing much. Asked about regulating carbon pollution, Trump characterized the Obama administration's actions as "an overreach that punishes rather than helps Americans" in the AEA questionnaire. He then went further. "Under my administration, all EPA rules will be reviewed. Any regulation that imposes undue costs on business enterprises will be eliminated."

He did not define what "undue cost" meant.

Renegotiating Paris

"If Donald Trump is elected, he would be the first climate-denying head of state in the world," the Sierra Club's executive director Michael Brune said on a Wednesday press call.

Trump has said he would seek to renegotiate the "one-sided," "bad," Paris climate agreement, ignoring the fact that the agreement is one-sided in favor of the United States, not against it. The rest of the planet has agreed to cut emissions, which will help to save Trump specifically from ruin, as someone who owns a lot of coastal property.

"The laws of physics are not very negotiable," James Murphy, senior counsel at the National Wildlife Federation, told ThinkProgress. He said that whether Trump would renegotiate the agreement or completely renege on it is immaterial to the fact that the United States should not walk away from the obligations it made at Paris.

Could Trump actually renegotiate the agreement? The future head of the U.N. climate office, Patricia Espinosa, said "it would not be easy." Yet unless the agreement gets locked in this year, he could certainly slow the process down or move to take America out of it as the Bush administration did with the Kyoto

Protocol 16 years ago. This could lead to similar defections from other countries.

"Trump is proposing we negotiate away American global leadership," Sierra Club's Shulman said. "What he said is ridiculous and would do irreparable damage to our role in the world. Trump's comments show how little he understands about conducting foreign policy."

Given how little regard Trump appears to hold for international agreements and U.S. allies, this may not hold much sway in a Trump administration.

Carbon and Energy in a Tax Compromise?

Cramer, Trump's energy adviser, made some waves last week when he said he advised Trump that he should consider a carbon tax as a replacement for the Clean Power Plan.

Trump replied on Twitter that reports that he might consider a carbon tax were false.

Indeed, Trump replied in the AEA questionnaire that he would not support a carbon tax, nor the administration's social cost of carbon.

It's possible a carbon tax could get folded into a broader tax compromise, but people say that all the time and it never happens. Trump could be different—his anti-corporate rhetoric alarmed the fossil fuel industry earlier in the campaign. Trump is expected to lay out a broadly fossil-fuel-friendly plan in his North Dakota speech, however.

"Trump believes that when oil spills occur 'you clean them up' and called the push to develop renewable energy a 'big mistake' and 'an expensive way of making treehuggers feel good about themselves,'" Shulman said. "The current GOP drive to subsidize fossil fuels at the expense of renewables would continue under a President Trump."

Extract, Baby, Extract

Trump has promised to bring back coal jobs when campaigning in West Virginia. Which is a problem when most of the coal jobs that have been lost were due to decisions made by the industry to mechanize their workforce. And the market is simply moving away from coal to natural gas and renewable energy. It's unclear what Trump would do on this, other than blow smoke.

That doesn't mean the coal industry isn't on board with a candidate who is alarmingly unfamiliar with the energy sector.

When coal executive Bob Murray suggested Trump allow more LNG terminals to export more natural gas, Trump had a question for Murray. "What's LNG?" Liquefied natural gas terminals are the only way to transport natural gas overseas, which would reduce the domestic natural gas supply glut and, at least to the coal industry, make coal more competitive. A president promising to bring coal jobs back should be familiar with the economic trends affecting coal.

Still, Murray was impressed with Trump. "He's got his head on right," Murray concluded after their meeting.

EIGHT

Politicians Have an Outsize Effect on the Environment

Andrea Thompson

> In the following viewpoint, Andrea Thompson expresses concern about President Donald Trump's disregard and even denial of the negative effects of human-influenced global warming. Through interviews with experts, Thompson explores why Trump's opponent Hillary Clinton was seen as the next great hope for the environment. Many scientists believed Clinton's environmental policies would be more in line with those of the scientific community. With an about-face in policy, what will be the effect on the environment? Thompson is a senior science writer at Climate Central, focusing on extreme weather and climate change.

The election of Donald Trump as the nation's next president spurred celebration in some quarters and dismay in others, including among those concerned about the steady warming of the planet.

The unrestrained emissions of heat-trapping greenhouse gases have altered the Earth's climate, raising sea levels, impacting ecosystems, and increasingly the likelihood of extreme weather. In terms of numbers, the world's temperature has risen by more than 1°F since 1900 and 2016 is expected to be the hottest year on record.

"Climate Experts Weigh in on Trump's Election Win," by Andrea Thompson, Climatecentral.org, November 9, 2016. Reprinted by permission.

Though climate change was not a major topic in much election coverage—there were no questions on it during the three presidential debates—many climate scientists and policy advocates supported Clinton. They expected that she would continue policies enacted by the Obama administration, such as the Clean Power Plan and the signing of international agreements to limit warming.

Trumps comments on climate change have included calling it a hoax and warning that Environmental Protection Agency policies are costing the country jobs, though he has talked about the importance of maintaining clean air and water. He has suggested he will pull out of the landmark Paris agreement and scuttle the Clean Power Plan, as well as boost the domestic coal and oil industries.

While the U.S. is only one country, it is a linchpin to the viability of international agreements and to moving the needle on limiting warming.

In response to Tuesday's landmark election, Climate Central reached out to climate, energy and policy researchers to see how they think a Trump presidency will impact climate research and efforts to limit future warming and mitigate what has already happened. We also asked what they think climate scientists should be doing in the coming weeks, months and years, including what they may personally be doing. Their answers have been lightly edited for clarity and brevity:

Jennifer Francis, sea ice researcher at Rutgers University

If President Trump acts on statements he made during the campaign, we are likely to see any federal efforts to curtail fossil fuel burning go up in smoke. I fear that funding for any scientific research related to the environment will be further cut by an unrestrained science-phobic Congress, even as we become ever more confident of the myriad ways that climate change is costing the U.S. economy billions of dollars, contributing to food and international insecurity, and disrupting daily life. As an optimist,

Temperatures have climbed in recent years around the globe, forcing areas not used to the heat to install cooling stations.

I hope that a President Trump will become more open-minded than the candidate Trump and allow facts to guide his presidential decisions. I also hope that as president he will take his grandchildren to visit our great national parks and see the beauty that will be destroyed if he ignores those facts.

Mother Nature did her share to influence this election by dishing up a smorgasbord of record-breaking heat, flooding, drought, and storms—yet, climate change was a non-issue. We know it's adversely affecting wildlife, agriculture, fisheries, outdoor sports, transportation, you name it—so clearly scientists of all stripes need to tell this story better. I will be redoubling my efforts to help people recognize impacts of climate change on their own lives, and also see the solutions that must happen to reduce the mess we leave for our children.

Jacquelyn Gill, paleoecologist at the University of Maine

We have just elected the only climate denying president in the free world, with a Young Earth Creationist vice president. It's hard to predict exactly how this will play out in terms of impacts to combat and mitigate against climate change, but one of the most immediate threats will be to the funding and agencies that support climate change research. Trump has gone on the record stating he'd cut funding for climate science, which will directly jeopardize ongoing efforts to understand how the climate system works, how to predict the impacts of climate change, and what the effective strategies for mitigation should be.

I worry that Trump's election will only rejuvenate the ongoing assault on climate scientists, both in terms of internet harassment and in Congress. In my opinion, scientists should be taking steps to protect the security of their online communications, their data, and their personal information. We should be supporting efforts like the Climate Legal Defense Fund. We should be careful about bringing new students into our labs while the future of science funding is so uncertain. We should be putting communication networks in place, reaching out to grant program officers, university administrators, and legislators, and doing what we can to advocate for the importance of our research and academic freedom at every level.

And even though it's scary, we need to be reaching out to the public, now more than ever. We need to find our own outreach communities and connect with those people, and to undertake efforts to humanize climate science. And we need to work with the folks who aren't scientists who are on the ground, on the front lines of climate change and climate justice, to make sure that we amplify their voices and pitch in where we can. This is going to be especially crucial for those of us who are in the most protected groups—white men especially.

Katharine Hayhoe, climate modeler at Texas Tech University

I work with cities, states, and provinces—helping them prepare for a changing climate, building resilience to the impacts we can't avoid, cutting carbon to reduce the impacts we can avoid. Cities like Washington, D.C., Chicago, and even tiny Georgetown, Texas, are at the forefront of this global movement. A president hostile to climate policy may be able to affect federal and even international action: but they can't stop cities and that's where the momentum is. That's what gives me hope.

Andrew Hoffman, sustainable development expert at the University of Michigan

Trump's election throws the future of environmental policy, both in the U.S. and globally, into confusion. His stated and tweeted positions on climate change, the Environmental Protection Agency, the Paris climate accord, the Clean Power Plan and many other related issues suggest that the future of much of the programs and policies of the past administration, indeed many from administrations going back to President Nixon's formation of the EPA, are in question. That said, Trump's positions have been uneven (for example, while deriding some environmental policies, he has endorsed programs by the National Wildlife Federation to protect the Great Lakes; announcing "let's make the Great Lakes great again") and some seem to have been hastily announced (such as his tweet that climate change is a Chinese plot). Let's wait and see how his positions solidify in the coming days of his administration. One aspect of Trump's campaign has been his unpredictability.

I would also add that I wrote an essay to warn that he may be following a similar path that Reagan started down and had to stop. Reagan tried to stop the actions of the EPA and faced a latent interest among the general public on the environment that was aroused by his disregard for environmental policies.

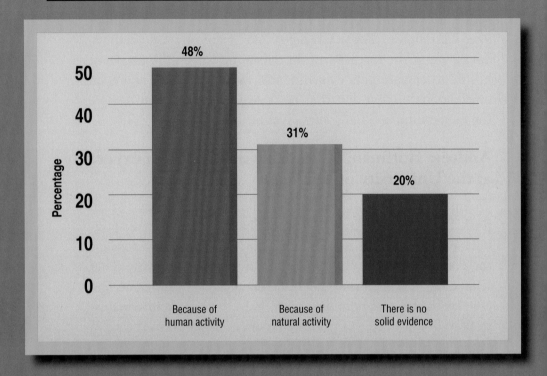

Percentage of Adults Who Believe Climate Change Is Due to Human Activity, Due to Natural Patterns, or Not Occurring

Source: Pew Research Center

Mark Jacobson, clean energy researcher at Stanford

I'm most concerned with how a Trump presidency will affect solutions to climate change, air pollution, and energy security. Fortunately, the cost of wind and solar are very low now and dropping still, and clean-energy technologies and startups are widespread, so we have momentum. At the state level, many states are moving to clean, renewable energy. It is still in the economic interest of Republicans and Democrats to expand clean, renewable energy. In fact, the five states with the highest fraction of electricity from wind are all "red" states that voted for Trump. Those countries that move faster toward clean, renewable energy will create more jobs, develop their economies faster, become more energy independent, reduce catastrophic risk, including terrorism, associated with centralized plants, and live healthier and longer, so this should be an incentive to keep moving in the right direction. Since most efforts to solve the problems have been at the state level over the past four years in any case (e.g., California, New York, and even inadvertently in Iowa and South Dakota with their expansion of wind), I am confident state and local steps can continue.

I will continue to do what I do, namely try to understand and solve the problems. There is nothing that an unsupportive president can do to stop my efforts.

Ralph Keeling, director of the CO_2 program at the Scripps Institution of Oceanography

It's not easy to formulate responses at this point. It's clearly too early to tell what Trump will do to change the landscape on climate mitigation. For now we will be waiting to see how much his policies will be guided by the sometimes extreme views that guided his campaign—such as being in denial of the climate problem. It's certainly easier to be in denial from the sidelines than from being in the driver's seat, so there's hope that a more reasoned approach will follow.

The main step for the climate scientists is to keep working on the science. If we end up on a slower track on mitigating climate change, this just means we need a faster track on adaptation and preparedness. There's a lot on the plate of the scientists regardless.

Michael Mann, paleoclimate researcher at Penn State

A Trump presidency might be game over for the climate. In other words, it might make it impossible to stabilize planetary warming below dangerous (i.e. greater than 2°C) levels. If Trump makes good on his campaign promises and pulls out of the Paris Treaty, it is difficult to see a path forward to keeping warming below dangerous levels.

It is time for introspection and contemplation. I'm still in the process of letting this sink in.

Laura Tam, sustainable development policy director at SPUR

As a policy analyst and advocate for local climate action, I can tell you that the urgency of sub-nationals and cities to take action to go fossil-free is even more important, and we should set up our systems to do this without the federal government, and perhaps in spite of it. The demonstration of the viability of 100 percent renewables for all energy needs can happen here in California and when we demonstrate the economic and environmental superiority of this model, the nation will not be long to follow. It will become inevitable. A Trump presidency will make local and state action even more urgent.

David Titley, climate and weather risk researcher at Penn State

Many black swans have taken flight this year. One thing science teaches you is that systems frequently revert to the mean. So, as dark as everything looks at this moment for fixing our climate, we need to have hope that we won't realize the worst case. If there is a silver lining it's that Trump does not seem bound by whatever he has said previously. So perhaps he will see the wisdom or at least self-interest, in investing in non-carbon, U.S.-produced, energy.

The climate community has a huge challenge ahead, to frame this issue in a way that will resonate with the likely president-elect. It may not be possible but it would be negligent to not even try.

NINE

We Need to Break Free from Dirty, Polluting Coal

Greenpeace

In the following viewpoint, Greenpeace provides a myriad of information supporting what is now considered a scientifically proven assertion that the coal industry plays a significant role in climate change and that only clean and renewable energy can help halt and reverse its negative effects. Unfortunately, coal is the planet's main global energy source. The authors emphatically state that the nations of the world must put the coal industry on its deathbed as part of the overall plan to ensure that global warming will not doom the planet. Greenpeace is a nongovernmental environmental organization.

The Problem: Coal Stokes Climate Warming

Coal is mainly made up of carbon, making it a carbon-intensive energy source. Burning coal produces nearly double the greenhouse gas emissions as burning gas, for the same amount of energy. So although coal generated less than 30 percent of the world's energy supply in 2013, it produced 46 percent of global carbon dioxide emissions.

A typical 500 MW coal power plant releases global warming emissions roughly equal to 600,000 cars. Yet unlike cars, coal plants are designed to operate for 40 years or more—a long lifespan of polluting energy.

Coal mining often produces the potent greenhouse gas methane. Methane is 84 times as powerful as carbon dioxide at disrupting the climate over a given 20-year period.

The use of coal as a power source has caused tremendous damage to the planet. Many global leaders are calling for an end to the use of coal and other dirty fossil fuels.

Coal's Dirty Plans—The Challenge We Must Meet

Total new coal generation capacity commissioned from 2010 to 2014 averaged 200 MW a day globally—further fuelling climate change. If plans for new coal-fired power plants around the world go ahead, carbon dioxide emissions from coal would balloon to 60 percent of the global total by 2030.

Worldwide proven coal reserves would allow us to burn it for 110 more years. Yet if even a small fraction of this dirty, polluting fuel is mined and burned, we have no chance to stay within 1.5 degrees Celsius of temperature rise. (Beyond this level of warming, many impacts of climate change become severe in some regions.)

Australia, China, India, Poland and South Africa are among countries using coal for more than two-thirds of their electricity and heat. South Africa sources 92 percent of its power from coal, and plans to add a further 16,400 MW by 2030.

Coal Is a Dying Industry

The tide has turned on coal. The 2015 Paris Agreement sent a clear signal that the era of fossil fuels—in particular coal—is coming to an end. Around the world, evidence grows of the coal industry's steep and irreversible decline.

- China: once accounting for half of all coal demand, in 2014 China's coal consumption levelled off, then fell rapidly. A war on pollution, renewable energy growth, and economic rebalancing are behind China's energy shift.

- Vietnam: although development plans in Southeast Asia formerly relied heavily on coal, Vietnam's 2016 decision to shelve plans for 70 large coal power plants suggests the shift to cleaner energy is gaining momentum.

- USA: coal production has fallen to the lowest level in three decades. Dozens of coal mining companies have filed for bankruptcy, including Peabody Energy, the world's biggest private coal miner.

- European Union: coal consumption has been falling since mid-2012, and the UK is committed to phasing out coal by 2025.

- India: although its coal production has been increasing rapidly, India's coal has ended up in stockpiles. Water shortages have led some plants to close. India has the world's four most polluted cities, and growing awareness of pollution has brought coal power's harmful effects to a head.

We Must Break Completely Free from Coal

The coal industry would have us think we need this dirty fuel to meet growing energy demand. This is simply untrue.

Greenpeace's respected Energy [R]evolution analyses show we can meet our energy needs through energy efficiency and a

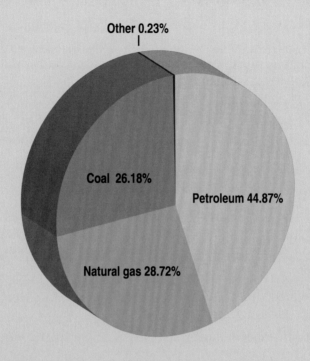

U.S. Energy-Related Carbon Dioxide Emissions by Major Fuel Source, 2016

Other 0.23%

Coal 26.18%

Petroleum 44.87%

Natural gas 28.72%

Source: https://www.eia.gov/tools/faqs/faq.php?id=75&t=11
U.S. Department of Energy, EIA

shift to 100 percent renewable energy.

We've already begun to change. The shift to safe and secure energy from the sun, wind and other clean sources now has unstoppable momentum.

We can't wait any longer to break free from coal. We know that to prevent catastrophic climate change, we must make the leap to 100 percent renewable energy as soon as possible.

What Greenpeace Is Doing to Fight Coal

Greenpeace is campaigning around the world to close down coal power plants and prevent construction of new ones.

The ways we help communities break free from coal include:

- highlighting coal's health impacts
- supporting farmers driven from their land to make way for construction of power plants
- campaigning to stop the flow of investment to coal and other fossil fuel projects.

Greenpeace also campaigns for clean renewable energy and other climate change solutions. And we expose the myths about false solutions, including expensive and unworkable carbon capture and storage.

What You Can Do

- Support a local action near you against a coal-fired power plant.
- Explore ways to power up your life with renewable energy.
- Call on your government to stop providing subsidies to fossil fuels.
- Divest from fossil fuels: make your own investments free of coal, oil and gas.

TEN

Scientists Are Concerned About the Coal Industry

Union of Concerned Scientists

> In the following excerpted viewpoint, the Union of Concerned Scientists details the various connections between coal and global warming. The UCS has been adamant about the need to rein in the advocates of the coal industry for the sake of the planet. The authors also examine how the coal industry negatively affects the environment and public health in other ways, including the polluting of our water. The Union of Concerned Scientists is a nonprofit science advocacy organization committed to developing and implementing innovative, practical solutions to some of the planet's most pressing problems.

Environmental and Public Health Impacts of Coal

Of the many environmental and public health risks associated with coal, the most serious in terms of its universal and potentially irreversible consequences is global warming. The scientific community has reached an overwhelming consensus that Earth's climate is warming—with potentially devastating future impacts—and that human activities such as the burning of fossil fuels and deforestation are largely to blame. Coal-fired power plants are the largest single source of CO_2 emissions in the United States, emitting as much as all modes of transportation combined in 2007.

The United States is not alone in this regard. China and India both are rapidly developing economically and plan on using their own very large reserves of coal to accelerate this process. While

"How Coal Works," Union of Concerned Scientists. Reprinted by permission.

Wind and solar power are clean energy sources that are considered to be kind to the environment and may hold the key to the future of the planet.

China is taking important steps to improve its energy efficiency and to build renewable sources of power, it has already passed the United States in annual CO_2 emissions, and is still set to expand its coal production much further. These trends make it even more important that the United States continue to invest in low-cost alternatives to coal and pass these technologies on to the developing world.

Beyond global warming, coal is responsible for countless environmental damages across the entire fuel cycle, from mining, to burning, to the disposal of waste products.

As discussed above, mining can lead to serious environmental impacts, including alteration of landscapes and resulting ecosystem destruction, water contamination, and human health and safety hazards. Mountaintop removal (MTR) mining has proven

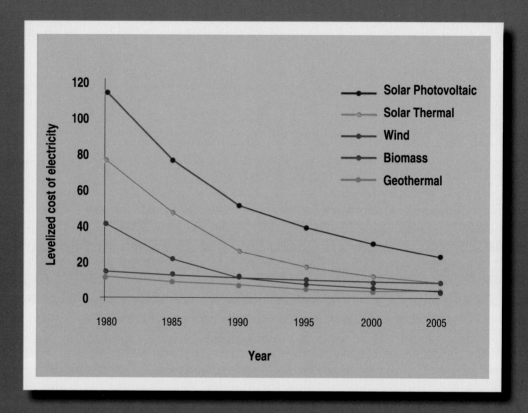

Cost of Renewable Electricity by Source, 1980–2005

Source: NREL Energy Analysis Office, via Union of Concerned Scientists

to be extremely destructive in this respect. Between 1985 and 2001, more than 7 percent of Appalachian forests were cut down and more than 1,200 miles of streams buried or polluted mining coal this way. In addition, black lung disease continues to kill about 1,000 former coal miners annually in the United States.

Impurities that are removed from coal before combustion are commonly stored in slurry reservoirs, where they pose great risks for nearby humans and the environment. There are over 700 such impoundments in Appalachia, and they may hold hundreds of millions of gallons of mine waste. Contaminants from these reservoirs can easily leach into surface and groundwater supplies. In extreme cases, the dams holding these reservoirs can fail, flooding local waterways and putting both wildlife and downstream communities at risk.

The nation's worst ever black water spill happened on October 11, 2000 near Inez, Kentucky. Just after midnight 306 million gallons of coal sludge, laced with coal cleaning chemicals and the heavy metals present in coal, leaked from a coal slurry impoundment at a Martin County Coal Company mountaintop removal site. The sludge leaked into an underground mine then burst out two portals into the Coldwater and Wolf Creeks. The Martin County slurry released 30 times more liquid than the Exxon Valdez.

Simply moving coal from one place to another has a significant environmental impact, with coal transportation accounting for about half of U.S. freight train traffic. These trains, as well as trucks and barges that transport coal, run on diesel—a major source of nitrogen oxide and soot.

The burning of coal creates some of the most damaging impacts. In addition to contributing to global warming through substantial emissions of carbon dioxide, coal plants give off the following pollutants:

- Sulfur dioxide, which produces acid rain. Coal combustion is the leading source of U.S. sulfur dioxide emissions.

- Nitrogen oxides, key contributors to ground-level ozone (smog) and respiratory illnesses.

- Particulate matter (soot), which produces haze and can cause chronic bronchitis, aggravated asthma, and premature death. (Both sulfur dioxide and nitrogen oxides transform into particulates in the atmosphere).

- Mercury, a neurotoxin that can contaminate waterways, make fish unsafe to eat, and cause birth defects. As with sulfur dioxide, coal burning is the leading source of mercury emissions in the U.S.

- Hydrocarbons, carbon monoxide, volatile organic compounds (VOCs), arsenic, lead, cadmium, and other toxic heavy metals.

After combustion, the remaining coal ash and sludge is often disposed of in unlined and unmonitored landfills and reservoirs. Heavy metals and toxic substances contained in this waste can contaminate drinking water supplies and harm local ecosystems. Even worse, failed reservoirs can flood coal waste into surrounding areas. In 2008, a Tennessee Valley Authority coal ash pond spilled into the nearby environment, requiring over $1 billion in estimated clean-up costs.

The Future of Coal

Coal is abundant in America, though not as abundant as previously thought. In 2007 the National Academy of Sciences reported that the country likely has at least a 100-year supply at today's consumption levels, but it could not confirm the often-quoted assertion that the nation has a 250-year supply of coal. Since then, the U.S. Geologic Survey substantially reduced its estimate of the amount of coal that is economically recoverable in the Powder River Basin, the nation's most important coal field. However, even if the U.S. coal reserve remains ample, other factors may limit coal use. With expected future limits on carbon dioxide emissions, production of coal will very likely have to decrease over time, in the absence of the success of carbon capture and sequestration on a large scale.

We are beginning to see signs already of the effect of expected future carbon dioxide regulations, and other policy and market changes, on the expansion of coal burning electricity. Power companies are starting to integrate the future price of carbon into their cost estimates for new plants, and this is seriously impacting their decisions over whether to build new coal plants. While there are still many coal plant proposals in the pipeline, over 100 coal plant proposals were cancelled or rejected by regulators in the last few years, in many cases in recognition of the financial risks posed by likely future carbon regulations.

Given the urgent need to dramatically reduce greenhouse gas emissions, and given coal power's enormous contribution to those emissions, options for reducing the CO_2 from coal plants are attracting increasing attention. As noted above, carbon capture and storage technology could play a significant role in reducing plant emissions in the future.

However, there are many currently available alternatives to coal power that would allow us to meet our energy needs and reduce our emissions of greenhouse gases and other pollutants. A 2009 UCS analysis (Climate 2030: A National Blueprint for a Clean Energy Economy) found that policies that promote more aggressive investments in energy efficiency and renewable energy would allow the United States to dramatically reduce its dependence on coal power—by about 85 percent relative by 2030 to what would be used under business-as-usual projections, while reducing power plant carbon emissions by 84 percent and saving consumers and businesses money.

ELEVEN

Catastrophic Rhetoric About Climate Change Is Baseless

Robert P. Murphy

> In the following viewpoint, Robert P. Murphy expresses skepticism about the dire warnings about climate change and argues that the predictions of doom for the planet have been greatly exaggerated. Concerned about the negative impact environmental regulations are destined to have on businesses, the author asserts that many journalists and others are promoting paranoia. Worse than their alarmist tendencies, he writes, is their tendency to deem climate science deniers as frauds who care little about humanity. Murphy is a senior economist specializing in climate change for the Institute for Energy Research.

As an economist studying climate change policy for several years, I often feel like I'm in the Twilight Zone. To listen to the constant drumbeat of catastrophic predictions based on the so-called scientific "consensus," and to witness the scathing denunciation of the "deniers" who are supposedly selling out humanity for money, you would certainly think that the periodic reports issued by the UN's Intergovernmental Panel on Climate Change (IPCC) would back up the alarmist rhetoric.

Yet I have found that the opposite is true. As I've documented over the years here at IER, all we have to do to defuse the alarmist position is quote from the UN's own documents, or from the

"Vox Features Yet Another Climate Science 'Denier,'" by Robert P. Murphy, Institute for Energy Research, May 27, 2015. Reprinted by permission.

Climate change skeptics point to recent blizzards as supposed evidence that global warming is a hoax.

reports issued by the Obama Administration's own teams. The baselessness of the catastrophic rhetoric is a secret hidden in plain sight, as it were. The people peddling paranoia are confident that not many Americans will actually read the compilations of the scientific literature, particularly the economic analyses comparing the costs and benefits of various proposed "solutions."

An excellent illustration of this mismatch between the alarmist rhetoric and the actual research is a recent Vox article by David Roberts. Much as an Old Testament prophet, Roberts comes to his readers with a depressing message: "The obvious truth about global warming is this: barring miracles, humanity is in for some awful [expletive]."

Since I just got through writing a post on MIT professor Robert Pindyck—who admits that the only case for aggressive action at

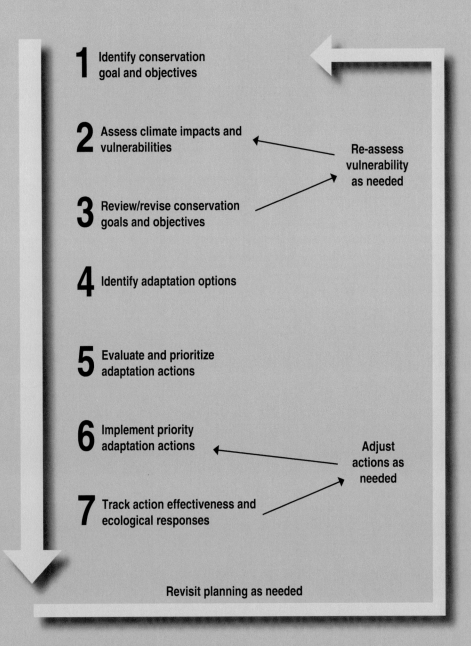

Creating, Planning, and Implementing an Adaption Plan

1 Identify conservation goal and objectives

2 Assess climate impacts and vulnerabilities

3 Review/revise conservation goals and objectives

Re-assess vulnerability as needed

4 Identify adaptation options

5 Evaluate and prioritize adaptation actions

6 Implement priority adaptation actions

Adjust actions as needed

7 Track action effectiveness and ecological responses

Revisit planning as needed

Source: Mount Shasta Bioregional Ecology Center

this point is to combat unlikely catastrophic scenarios that will probably not happen even if governments do nothing—I was curious to see how the Vox writer could possibly have come up with the opposite conclusion. In the rest of this post, I'll show a few of the problems with his analysis. The whole episode shows the neutral outsider how to be careful when navigating the rhetoric in the climate change debate.

Problem #1: Confusion Over "Business as Usual"

The first major problem in Roberts' Vox piece is his inaccurate description of the various climate scenarios contained in the latest IPCC report. Roberts's commentary of a chart in the Fifth Assessment Report (AR5) reads, "The black line is carbon emissions to date. The red line is the status quo — a projection of where emissions will go if no new substantial policy is passed to restrain greenhouse gas emissions."

This description of the Representative Concentration Pathways (RCPs) from the latest IPCC report is very misleading. However, I'm not really upset with Roberts, because when the AR5 report came out—with these RCPs instead of the previous Special Report on Emissions Scenarios (SRES)—I knew that people were going to assume that RCP8.5 represented "business as usual," in other words as the default outcome if humanity continued on its present path. So we can't really blame Roberts for telling Vox readers that that top line shows what will happen if governments do nothing; that's exactly the (inaccurate) conclusion that any quick reader would take away from the diagram. It's precisely for this reason that I was so disappointed when I saw the new IPCC AR5 report and how they had changed the way they classified future emission scenarios.

The specific problem is that the top line in the chart is a very high end estimate of future emissions under a "business as usual" scenario. As Texas A&M Regents Professor of Atmospheric Sciences John Nielsen-Gammon explains in a post on the Climate Change National Forum, the RCP8.5 scenario from the latest IPCC report relies on extreme assumptions regarding population growth, the delay in technological development, and so on. He cites a 2011 paper from the literature which found that "RCP8.5 comes in around the 90th percentile of published business-as-usual (or equivalently, baseline) scenarios, so it is higher than most business-as-usual scenarios."

In other words, if you study the literature of climate change and the various emission scenarios regarding "business as usual" where governments do not enact major policy changes, then some 90 percent involve lower emissions and hence lower global warming than the RCP8.5 scenario in the graph. It is therefore misleading when the first plank in David Roberts' Vox argument is to say matter-of-factly that humanity will experience the RCP8.5 outcome, absent aggressive government action.

The interested reader should consult Nielsen-Gammon's post for all the nuances, but his overall conclusion is that a more accurate "business as usual" trajectory would fall in between the RCP6 and RCP8.5 pathways in the graph above, and his best guess is that with no government intervention, the globe will warm an additional 3 degrees Celsius by 2100 (meaning a total of 3.6°C warming since preindustrial times). I want to stress that Nielsen-Gammon isn't challenging the IPCC report's range of estimated "climate sensitivity" or other parameters. All Nielsen-Gammon is doing is trying to fit the scientific findings summarized in the latest report, in the context of the traditional estimates of future emission scenarios in the literature (and as outlined in the previous IPCC reports).

Problem #2: Quoting a Non-Expert for Hard and Fast Conclusions

In the previous section we showed that David Roberts got off to a shaky start by misrepresenting (probably innocently) what the "consensus" projections are for emissions and global warming if governments take no major actions going forward. But the next step in his argument—going from (exaggerated) warming to impacts on humanity—is also dubious. Here's Roberts:

We recently passed 400 parts per million of CO_2 in the atmosphere; the status quo will take us up to 1,000 ppm, raising global average temperature (from a pre-industrial baseline) between 3.2 and 5.4 degrees Celsius. That will mean, according to a 2012 World Bank report, "extreme heat-waves, declining global food stocks, loss of ecosystems and biodiversity, and life-threatening sea level rise," the effects of which will be "tilted against many of the world's poorest regions," stalling or reversing decades of development work. "A 4°C warmer world can, and must be, avoided," said the World Bank president.

But that's where we're headed. It will take enormous effort just to avoid that fate. Holding temperature down under 2°C—the widely agreed upon target—would require an utterly unprecedented level of global mobilization and coordination, sustained over decades. There's no sign of that happening, or reason to think it's plausible anytime soon. And so, awful [expletive] it is.

To repeat, it is not accurate in the above quotation for Roberts to say "the status quo will take us up to 1,000 ppm," because that assumes the RCP8.5 scenario is the status quo—which it is not. More reasonable, middle-of-the-road projections would put the concentration in the year 2100 below that level, so that even stipulating everything else in the latest IPCC report, we would not expect the level of warming that Roberts proposes in his piece.

However, let's consider the next link in his argument. To show us just how unacceptable this stipulated status quo warming would be, Roberts doesn't refer to the latest "consensus" science on estimated impacts from climate change in the AR5 Working Group II report—which came out in March 2014. Instead, Roberts refers to a 2012 report from the World Bank, and quotes from the president of the World Bank to get his money line on just how little hope remains for humanity.

Now don't get me wrong, the president of the World Bank, Dr. Jim Yong Kim, is a really smart guy—he has an MD and a PhD in anthropology from Harvard. But it's odd that the bulk of Roberts' case comes from the summary provided by someone who is not trained in climate science, referring to a World Bank report from three years ago.

In contrast to the horrible picture painted by Roberts in his Vox piece, one of the three computer models selected by the Obama Administration for modeling future impacts of climate change concluded that there would be net benefits to humanity from global warming, up through about 3°C. There really haven't been many comprehensive studies estimating the impacts on humanity from warming above 3°C. There is a study by Maddison and Rehdanz (in 2011) showing a very large impact, but it is clearly an outlier, well beyond the rest of the literature. Furthermore, the last item in the table—referring to a 2012 study by Roson and van der Mensbrugghe—projects that 4.9°C of global warming would merely reduce global GDP by 4.6 percent.

How should we think about that type of impact? Is that catastrophic? Is that worth mobilizing the entire globe to combat? Is such a threat one of the most important issues of our day?

Well, the very same AR5 report from the IPCC estimates that to keep global warming contained to 2°C, governments around the world would need to implement policies that would cause economic damage of 4.8 percent of global consumption in the year 2100.

To summarize, the latest IPCC report shows that in a middle-of-the-road outcome, the total damage to humanity from governments implementing a popular climate goal target (namely, limiting warming to 2°C) is greater than the total damage to humanity from unrestricted global warming.

This is why I say the climate change debate feels like the Twilight Zone to me: The advocates for aggressive government intervention go through this whole production of soliciting input from various scientists and economists around the world, and when all is said and done their own report shows that the most likely outcome is that "doing nothing" stacks up nicely against other possible strategies.

Roberts Admits Scientists Are Playing Politics

Now in fairness, I'm sure David Roberts or other proponents of massive government intervention could come back and say something like, "Sure, there aren't comprehensive studies quantifying the exact global impacts from unrestricted emissions. But we have an idea of how bad things might be for particular groups of people or regions of the globe, and that's what we're talking about with our alarmist rhetoric."

Well, nobody can prove that a catastrophe won't happen, but readers should be on their guard when ostensible experts just start throwing out qualitative warnings without providing precise scientific reasons for their alarm bells. To back up my claim, all I have to do is quote from…David Roberts' own Vox piece. Look at his incredibly candid discussion of how political and non-objective the supposed scientific experts have been, when telling the public the "truth" about climate change:

> The latest contretemps was sparked by a comment in Nature by Oliver Geden….Politicians, he says, want good news. They want to hear that it is still possible to limit temperature to 2°C. Even more, they want to hear that they can do so while avoiding aggressive emission cuts in the near-term—say, until they're out of office.
>
> Climate scientists, Geden says, feel pressure to provide the good news. They're worried that if they don't, if they come off as "alarmist" or hectoring, they will simply be ignored, boxed out of the debate. And so they construct models showing that it is possible to hit the 2°C target. The message is always, "We're running out of time; we've only got five or 10 years to turn things around, but we can do it if we put our minds to it."
>
> That was the message in 1990, in 2000, in 2010. How can we still have five or 10 years left? The answer, Geden says, is that scientists are baking increasingly unrealistic assumptions into their models.

Even though Roberts and I are (obviously) coming to this issue from completely different points, I respect his honesty in printing the above. (At least one leading alarmist climate scientist bit his head off for doing so.) Although Roberts, citing Oliver Geden, thinks the climate scientists are being pressured by politicians to paint a rosy picture that justifies aggressive government climate policy, the important point I want to emphasize is: Roberts in his Vox piece is claiming matter of factly that scientists keep tweaking their models to produce results that politicians want to hear. That's part of the message we at IER have been telling Americans for years, and yet when we say it, we are called "deniers" who reject the "scientific consensus."

Conclusion

Although it's the opposite of what he intended, David Roberts' Vox article on the climate debate underscores that the published literature on climate change does not justify the typical policy recommendations being pushed on the public and government officials. Roberts openly admits that the supposedly objective scientists are deliberately altering their assumptions time and again, to keep the output of their "models" on point and saying what the politicians want to hear. It's refreshing when someone from "the other side" of this debate is so frank about the type of process producing the fodder which is then rushed to Capitol Hill as evidence for massive tax hikes and regulations on industry.

TWELVE

A Multitude of Factors Affect Our Climate's Future

Robert Kopp

> In the following viewpoint, Robert Kopp shares his expertise about the effects of the American withdrawal from the Paris Agreement. His warning that the nations of the world have not gone far enough to combat global warming is tied to his belief that the move by President Trump, while harmful, will likely not make matters significantly worse. Kopp argues both the viewpoints of optimists and pessimists before concluding that one must tie the economic and environmental impact of plans such as that agreed upon in Paris to best judge their soundness. Kopp is a professor in the Department of Earth and Planetary Sciences and director of the Coastal Climate Risk and Resilience Initiative at Rutgers University.

Even before the Paris Agreement was signed in December 2015, market forces and policy measures were starting to tilt the world toward a lower-carbon future. U.S. carbon dioxide emissions peaked in 2007, and Chinese emissions may have peaked in 2014. Solar energy, wind and energy storage are expanding rapidly.

Yet as a climate scientist and a climate policy scholar, I know market forces and current policies are far from adequate to limit the rise in global temperatures, as envisioned in the Paris Agreement.

"How Bad Could Trump's Paris Agreement Withdrawal Be? A Scientist's Perspective," by Robert Kopp, *The Conversation*, June 1, 2017. https://theconversation.com/how-bad-could-trumps-paris-agreement-withdrawal-be-a-scientists-perspective-78721?sa=-google&sq=trump+paris+accord&sr=1. Licensed under CC BY 4.0 International.

And so the Trump administration's decision to withdraw from the Paris Agreement could have a range of consequences for the United States and for humanity. But how broad will these impacts be?

Part of the uncertainty stems from how the climate system will respond to humanity's greenhouse gas emissions. If we are lucky, the climate will be less sensitive than scientists think is most likely; if we are unlucky, it will be more sensitive. But most of the uncertainty arises from how the 194 other signatories of the Paris Agreement and the global economy will respond to Trump's decision.

The Optimist's Case

The Paris Agreement's long-term goal is to limit global warming to 1.5 to 2.0 degrees Celsius (2.7 to 3.6 degrees Fahrenheit) above preindustrial temperatures, or about 0.5 to 1.0 degrees C (0.9 to 1.8 degrees F) above the current global average temperature.

Current policies in the U.S., even without the power plant regulations proposed by the Obama administration, are adequate to reduce greenhouse gas emissions to about 16 percent below 2005 levels by 2020. But significant new policies at the federal and state level are necessary to meet the U.S. commitment under the Paris Agreement to lower its emissions to 26 percent to 28 percent below 2005 levels by 2025. Largely independent of Trump's decision to withdraw from the Paris Agreement, his obstruction of federal policy to cut greenhouse gas emissions means these targets are not likely to be met.

Meanwhile, however, China and Europe appear to be ready to take up the mantle of climate leadership that the U.S. is abdicating. And so if the U.S. departure from the Paris Agreement does not disrupt international progress, then Trump's move may prove largely symbolic. (Indeed, under the terms of the Paris Agreement, the departure will not take effect until November 4, 2020—a day after the next presidential election.) Nonetheless, U.S. industry may suffer and the U.S. reputation as a reliable diplomatic partner certainly will.

It's our planet; we should care what happens to it! Get involved in projects and clubs at school to learn more about what our leaders have planned for the environment.

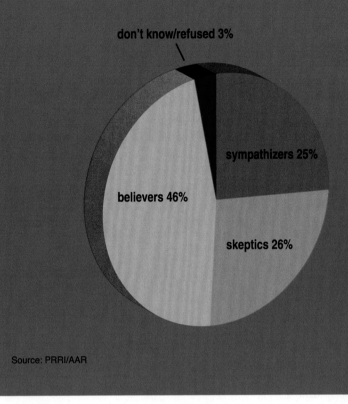

Climate Change Factions in the U.S., 2014

don't know/refused 3%

sympathizers 25%

believers 46%

skeptics 26%

Source: PRRI/AAR

But the planet will not notice much. Over the five years between 2020 and 2025, the U.S. will emit a total of about 2.5 billion more tons of carbon dioxide-equivalent greenhouse gases than it would if it got on a path to meet its 2025 goal. That's about the same as a 6 percent increase in one year's worth of global carbon dioxide emissions.

Until recently, the federal government used an estimate of the social cost of carbon dioxide—one way to calculate the damage caused by climate change—of about US$40/ton. Based on that estimate, the additional emissions caused by the U.S. failing to meet its Paris commitment would cause about $100 billion of damage to the global economy—not an insignificant number, but small in comparison to the size of the global economy. If state governments in California and elsewhere pick up some of the slack left by federal abdication, as some governors are pledging they will, the damage will be less.

If, after Trump, the U.S. rejoins a healthy global climate regime and shifts with a few years' delay on to an emissions trajectory consistent with Paris' long-term goals, then the climate will not be much harmed by any transient U.S. lethargy. The main damage will have been to U.S. leadership, in the clean energy industry and in the world at large.

The Pessimist's Case

However, the Paris Agreement would not have happened without U.S. leadership. Perhaps, despite the efforts of China and Europe, it will fall apart without the U.S.

President Trump has talked often about reopening coal mines. This is unlikely to happen without significant subsidies – coal is in general no longer competitive as an electricity source with natural gas or, increasingly, solar or wind energy.

But if Trump's vision of a "canceled" Paris Agreement and booming coal economy were to be realized, an analysis my colleagues and I did shows that the costs to the U.S. could be severe. As I wrote in August:

> By the middle of the century, climate models indicate that global mean temperature would likely be about 0.5–1.6 degrees F warmer than today under the Paris Path, but 1.6–3.1 degrees F warmer under the Trump Trajectory. The models also show that, by the last two decades of this century, temperatures would have stabilized under the Paris Path, while the Trump Trajectory would likely be about 4.4–8.5 degrees F warmer.
>
> Sea-level projections by the Intergovernmental Panel on Climate Change (IPCC), by our research group and by others indicate that global average sea level at the end of the century would likely be about 1–2.5 feet higher under the Paris path than in 2000.
>
> Emerging science about the instability of the Antarctic ice sheet suggests it might be around three to six feet higher—or

even more—under the Trump trajectory. And, due to the slow response of the ocean and ice sheets to changes in temperatures, the Trump trajectory would lock in many more feet of sea-level rise over the coming centuries—quite possibly more than 30 feet.

Quantitative risk analyses show that warming would impose costs on human health, on agriculture and on the energy system. It would increase the risk of civil conflict globally. And rising seas would reshape coastlines around the U.S. and around the world.

The Ultra-pessimist's Case

The pessimist's case assumes that future catastrophes will come from the climate and its effects. The ultra-pessimist looks elsewhere.

The Paris Agreement is a milestone agreement within a cooperative system of global governance in which organizations like NATO, the United Nations and the European Union play key roles—a system which some of President Trump's key advisers seek to undermine.

If isolationist policies, including pulling out of the Paris Agreement and weakening the Western alliance, lead to a global trade war and thence to an economic depression, the shutdown of significant chunks of the economy could lead to a larger reduction in greenhouse gas emissions than any careful, deliberate decarbonization policy.

The U.S. saw a small version of this between 2007 and 2009, when the economic downturn was the primary driver of a 10 percent drop in U.S. emissions. Most economic models, including those used to produce projections of future greenhouse gas emissions, are not capable of modeling abrupt changes such as these.

Ironically, Trump's decision to withdrawal from global governance, including the Paris Agreement, would in this scenario lower emissions. But global depression is one of the most harmful ways possible to do that—one that would inflict great hardship on the American workers Trump purports to help.

What You Should Know About Our Climate's Future

Facts About Climate Change

- Human activities such as burning fossil fuels and chopping down the trees in forests have caused global warming and shifts in normal climate patterns, causing more severe weather outbreaks.

- Hotter air causes increased ocean evaporation. The result is stronger heat waves and more intense storms. The number of natural disasters has nearly doubled in recent decades, and 90 percent of them have been weather-related.

- Among the consequences of changing conditions have been dying coral reefs and the loss of sea ice that Arctic animals had called home.

- The concentration of carbon dioxide in Earth's atmosphere in 2016 was at its highest level in more than three million years.

- The highest global temperatures ever were recorded in 2016, marking the third straight year in which such a dubious record was established.

- About 11 percent of all global greenhouse gas emissions resulted from the loss of forest land. That is comparable to the amount of gas emissions caused by every car and truck on the planet.

- An estimated 800 million people are currently vulnerable to climate change threats such as droughts, floods, heat waves, and extreme weather events such as tsunamis and hurricanes.

- Less than one percent of all the forest lands in the world are coastal, but they store more than five times the carbon as do tropical forests.

- An area of coastal ecosystems larger than New York City is destroyed every year, releasing carbon into the air and resulting in increased extreme weather threats for coastal communities globally.

- Saving tropical forests that store carbon is estimated to solve about 30 percent of the global warming problem on the planet. But this issue receives only 2 percent of the funding that goes into the overall research and development in the battle against climate change.

- Nearly two hundred countries signed off on the Paris Agreement that, in part, sought to lower global temperatures by reducing gas emissions.

- The United States was one of the countries that signed the Paris Agreement during the Obama administration. But successor Donald Trump claimed business unfairness and pulled the country out of the landmark deal.

- It would take an estimated $140 billion to make all the changes needed to save humanity from global warming. That is only 0.1 percent of the global gross domestic product (GDP), indicating that it is quite financially feasible.

- The Amazon rain forest, which is among the greatest life-support systems on the planet, has been threatened. A group called Conservation International is working to achieve zero-net deforestation there by the year 2020.

- All but one of the sixteen hottest years on the planet since temperatures have been recorded over the last 134 years has occurred since the year 2000, thereby proving the validity of global warming. Many scientists claim that the average global temperature could rise by 10 degrees

Fahrenheit over the next century if successful solutions are not put in place and achieved.

- The burning of fossil fuels is the largest source of heat-trapping pollution in the United States, producing about two billion tons of carbon dioxide released into the atmosphere every year. Coal-burning power plants are by far the greatest contributor.

- The trapping of heat when carbon dioxide and other pollutants are emitted into the air is what is known as the "greenhouse effect."

- President Trump cited a need to promote jobs in the coal industry as one reason for pulling the United States out of the Paris Agreement. But many have debated that the number of such jobs that can be created do not compare to the damage the coal industry does to the environment.

- Those who disagree with the policies of Donald Trump in regard to the coal industry argue that money should be placed into training coal miners to work in clean energy fields, thereby making the country less dependent on coal and allowing the United States to return to the Paris Agreement and do its part in the battle against climate change.

- Scientists estimated that about one-fifth of the cause for the 2015 drought in California—its worst on record—was global warming. Those same scientists claimed that the chances for similar water shortages have doubled over the past century.

- The number and intensity of powerful North Atlantic hurricanes has increased since the 1980s, according to scientists.

- Scientists now assert with certainty that weather events such as heat waves can be directly attributed to global warming.

- Antarctica has been losing about 134 million metric tons

of ice per year since 2002. That means the melting of ice caps and rising sea levels, resulting in catastrophic events for heavily populated coastal areas.

- Extreme heat waves have caused tens of thousands of deaths in recent years. Some areas of the world, such as in northern and central Africa, might not be able to survive worsening conditions if global warming is not halted and reversed.

- Severe droughts have resulted in an increased number of wildfires in the western United States.

- The disruption of habitats such as coral reefs is expected to drive many plant and animal species to extinction.

- China surpassed the United States at one point as a global pollutant, but its inclusion in the Paris Agreement and recent efforts to strongly curb and even eliminate its greenhouse gas emissions have resulted in major positive changes in that country.

- Though the United States makes up just 4 percent of the world population, it produces about 16 percent of all its carbon dioxide pollutants. That equals the percentage of the European Union and India combined.

- The coal industry embraced by President Trump is considered the greatest threat to the environment. That is why China has taken dramatic steps to curb and eventually eliminate its dependence on coal.

- The United States Environmental Protection Agency in 2015 pledged to reduce carbon emissions back to 2005 levels by the year 2030 through its Clean Power Plan. But President Trump has worked to reverse the initiative due to what he perceives as bad business practices.

- Solar and wind power produced more than 5 percent of all electricity in the United States in 2015 for the first time ever.

- The Obama administration vowed to contribute $3 billion

to the Green Climate Fund to help poor countries adapt to changes necessary to reverse climate change. But Donald Trump has vowed to kill the initiative.

- Global sea level rose about eight inches during the twentieth century. The rate of that sea level rise has nearly doubled during the first two decades of this century.

- Glaciers are melting nearly everywhere on the planet—including in the Alps, Himalayas, Andes, Rockies, Alaska, and Africa.

- Views from satellites have shown that the amount of spring snow cover in the Northern Hemisphere has decreased over the past five decades. It has also revealed that the snow is melting earlier.

- Glacier National Park in Montana currently boasts only 25 glaciers whereas it featured 150 in 2010.

- More than one million species have already become extinct due to disappearing habitats caused by global warming.

- Since the Industrial Revolution was launched around 1700, the amount of carbon pollutants emitted into the atmosphere has risen about 34 percent.

What You Should Do About Our Climate's Future

Though many skeptics remain, the majority of Americans believe that climate change is real. They accept the consensus that human activity is greatly to blame for global warming. They also see it as a threat to the planet.

But they also perceive the problem to be bigger than they are. They shrug their shoulders and think to themselves that climate change is an issue that only world leaders and expert scientists can solve. And to some extent they are right. If those in power do not recognize the threat and take drastic steps to lower global temperatures through environmental policy, the problem will likely worsen.

Yet the average person is not powerless. Those who learn the steps they can take to contribute soon realize they too can play a role in stopping and reversing global warming. If halting the effects of climate change is indeed a worldwide campaign, everyone in the world should feel such an obligation.

Some of the steps could be considered sacrifices. Among them is to become a vegetarian. The Worldwatch Institute has estimated that the share of greenhouse gas emissions from animal agriculture runs as high as 51 percent. Though other assessments are lower, there is no doubt that the meat industry contributes to the problem. Those who believe refusing to eat meat presents too great a challenge could go vegetarian once or twice a week to show solidarity with the green movement.

Consuming organic rather than chemically laced foods should also be part of the plan. That will keep pesticides and food grown with synthetic fertilizers out of the body. Such fertilizers are created through oil refining, which means even buying a nonorganic piece of fruit is doing big oil companies that pollute a small favor.

Buying from nearby stores that produce their own goods or purchase them locally helps in more ways than one. It often allows you to walk or ride a bike to buy items, which saves car fuel. It also promotes a business that doesn't use cars or trucks that travel long distances to ship material to it.

Such energy-saving exercises should be shared with friends and family. The more people who can be motivated to carry out tasks that will prove beneficial to the environment, the greater impact one can make. For instance, four people doing the same things quadruples the positive impact on climate change.

One move that can help save the planet is hanging clothes on a line. After all, dryers burn fossil fuel. And clothes dried by the sun and fresh air last longer, which in turn keeps new clothes from being shipped by trucks and freighters that burn oil. There's nothing like the freshness of clothes dried outdoors. It's more time-consuming, but it can be worth it.

So can riding a bike or taking a walk. Every opportunity to avoid car travel should be embraced. If a destination is within walking or biking distance and the weather is conducive, take a walk or take a bike. It not only helps save the environment, but it is far healthier for the human body than sitting in a car watching the telephone poles go by. One should encourage friends and family members to walk or bike whenever possible.

One should not allow their parents to fall into the trap of using their children as an excuse to increase carbon emissions by buying meat products and driving them wherever they need to go. What is convenient is often not friendly to the environment. Making clear to parents that one is willing to eat organically grown fruits and vegetables and eschew car rides for walking and biking can make the youth of America important cogs in the battle against global warming.

So can a commitment to such basics as recycling and clean energy. Understanding what is recyclable and what is not allows one to recycle everything that is allowed and reduces the number of new products that are made from scratch.

Trying to convince parents to purchase solar panels that absorb sunlight to produce energy for the home might elicit a groan about the cost of such an endeavor. But the effort will be worthwhile if they are informed that not only will solar panels benefit the environment, they will also eventually save money on energy bills.

Doing what one can individually is important. But involving friends, family members, and others in a community effort can help far more in the fight against global warming. And it makes one feel good to know that he or she is contributing to what some believe is the most important battle of our time. That is, the battle to save Planet Earth.

The editors have compiled the following list of organizations concerned with the issues debated in this book. The descriptions are derived from materials provided by the organizations. All have publications or information available for interested readers. The list was compiled on the date of publication of the present volume; the information provided here may change. Be aware that many organizations take several weeks or longer to respond to inquiries, so allow as much time as possible.

350.org

20 Jay Street
Suite 732
Brooklyn, NY 11201
(646) 801-0759
email: feedback@350.org
website: https://350.org

This organization works to combat the fossil fuel industry. Its effort is focused on stopping all new coal, oil, and gas projects while promoting clean energy.

Alliance for Climate Education

4696 Broadway
Suite 2
Boulder, CO 80304
(720) 383-7129
website: https://acespace.org

This organization seeks to educate high school students about climate change. It takes steps to empower young people to work toward positive solutions.

The Climate Reality Project

email: info@carthagegroup.com
website: http://www.algore.com/project/the-climate-reality-project

Led by former vice president Al Gore, the Climate Reality Project works to bring people together to demand stronger political action against global warming. The group supports action around the world.

Environmental Defense Fund
1875 Connecticut Avenue NW
Suite 600
Washington, DC 20009
(800) 684-3322
website: http://www.edf.org

The EDF is guided by both science and economics. Its mission is to find practical and sustainable solutions to the most pressing and serious environmental problems.

Greenpeace USA
702 8th Street NW
Suite 300
Washington, DC 20001
(800) 722-6995
email: info@wdc.greenpeace.org
website: http://www.greenpeace.org/usa

Greenpeace touts itself as the leading independent campaigning organization using peaceful protest to expose global environmental problems and promote solutions essential to a green and peaceful future.

Natural Resources Defense Council
40 West 20th Street
11th Floor
New York, NY 10011
(212) 727-2700
email: nrdcinfo@nrdc.org
website: https://www.nrdc.org

The NRDC works to safeguard the earth—its people, plants, and animals. Its mission is to protect the natural systems on which all life depends.

The Sierra Club
2101 Webster Street
Suite 1300
Oakland, CA 94612
(415) 977-5500
email: information@sierraclub.org
website: http://affa-sc.org/contact

An organization with more than three million members, the Sierra Club seeks to protect wildlife and the environment. Its efforts have helped pass the Clean Air Act, Clean Water Act, and Endangered Species Act.

Union of Concerned Scientists
Two Battle Square
Cambridge, MA 02138-3780
(617) 547-5552
website: http://www.ucsusa.org

The scientists that make up this organization work to implement practical and creative solutions to world problems. Included are combatting global warming and developing sustainable ways to feed, power, and transport people.

BIBLIOGRAPHY

Books

Michael C. Enwerem, *The Paris Agreement on Climate Change: A Better Chance to Tackling Global Climate Change*. Colorado Springs, CO: CreateSpace Independent Publishing Platform, 2016.

The author of this book expresses optimism over the Paris Agreement and how the nations of the world came together to acknowledge the effects of climate change and to commit to turn away from fossil fuels.

Paul Hawken, *Drawdown: The Most Comprehensive Plan Ever Proposed to Reverse Global Warming*. New York, NY: Penguin Books, 2017.

Hawken is an activist who explains a detailed plan to reverse the effects of global warming and achieve a healthier planet.

Naomi Klein, *This Changes Everything: Capitalism vs. The Climate*. New York, NY: Simon & Schuster, 2015.

This book makes the argument that the current state of capitalism cannot coexist with ending global warming. It asserts that changes must be made to the free market system to achieve victory in the battle against climate change.

Elizabeth Kolbert, *The Sixth Extinction: An Unnatural History*. New York, NY: Picador Publishing, 2015.

This top bestseller explains that by burning fossil fuels that change the atmosphere, oceans, and climate, humankind is threatening the existence of millions of animal species. This book even received a sparkling review from President Barack Obama.

Bruno Manser, *Voices from the Rainforest: Testimonies of a Threatened People*. Strategic Development and Research Development Centre, 2015.

This book tells the story of logging in the rain forest and how it has devastated the native people. It further explains how governments that have encouraged the industry have contributed to the suffering of the indigenous people.

Edmond Mathez, *Climate Change: The Science of Global Warming and Our Energy Future*. New York, NY: Columbia University Press, 2009.
This book explains the basic science behind the natural progress of climate change and the effect human activity has had on the worsening situation on the planet.

Dr. Jerome Patoux, *Science of Climate: Global Warming and Climate Change*. Colorado Springs, CO: CreateSpace Independent Publishing Platform, 2016.
This book allows students to understand the reality of global warming and explore the greenhouse effect and greenhouse gases. It also describes the role played by humankind in sending the gases into the atmosphere.

Gavin Schmits and Joshua Wolfe, *Climate Change: Picturing the Science*. New York, NY: W.W. Norton, 2009.
The authors seek to teach readers about human-induced climate change through pictures and their expertise. Their goal is to further global cooperation in adopting new, sustainable ways of living.

Jan Zalasieewicz and Mark Wlliams, *The Goldilocks Planet: The 4 Billion Year Story of Earth's Climate*. New York, NY: Oxford University Press, 2013.
The dramatic and abrupt history of how the earth's climate has changed is explained. The planet has experienced bitterly cold and sweltering hot temperatures that have greatly impacted the plant and animal communities.

Periodicals and Internet Sources

Tim Appenzeller and Dennis R. Dimick, "Signs from Earth," *National Geographic*. http://ngm.nationalgeographic.com /ngm/0409/feature1/.

Democracy in America, "The Flaws in Donald Trump's Decision to Pull Out of the Paris Accord," *Economist*, June 1, 2017. https://www.economist.com/blogs/democracyinamerica/ 2017/06/america-and-climate-change.

Fiona Harvey, "Arctic Ice Melt Could Trigger Uncontrollable Climate Change at Global Level," *Guardian*, November 25, 2016. https://www.theguardian.com/environment/2016/nov /25/arctic-ice-melt-trigger-uncontrollable-climate- change-global-level.

Max Kutner, "Trump Called Global Warming a 'Hoax.'
This Converted Skeptic Could Change That,"
Newsweek, June 6, 2017. http://www.newsweek.com/
trump-global-warming-hoax-paris-berkeley-621073.

Stephen Leahy, "By 2100, Deadly Heat May Threaten
Majority of Humankind," *National Geographic*, June 19,
2017. http://news.nationalgeographic.com/2017/06/
heatwaves-climate-change-global-warming/.

Amanda MacMillan, "Global Warming 101," NRDC.org, March
11, 2016. https://www.nrdc.org/stories/global-warming-101?g-
clid=CL-nh7Tp5dQCFQW2wAode8oMjg.

Brendan Mahoney, "How Rain Forest Destruction Affects You,"
Pendulum, 2009. http://www.elon.edu/e-web/pendulum/
issues/2006/08_31/opinions/rainforest.xhtml.

Bill McKibben, "A World at War: We're Under Attack from
Climate Change—and Our Only Hope Is to Mobilize Like
We Did in WWII," *New Republic*, August 15, 2006. https://
newrepublic.com/article/135684/declare-war-
climate-change-mobilize-wwii.

Brad Plumer and Nadja Popovich, "As Climate Changes,
Southern States Will Suffer More than Others," *New York
Times*, June 29, 2017. https://www.nytimes.com/interac-
tive/2017/06/29/climate/southern-states-worse-
climate-effects.html?rref=collection%2Fsection
collection%2Fclimate&action=click&contentCollection
=climate&region=rank&module=package&version=
highlights&contentPlacement=1&pgtype=sectionfront.

Tim Radford, "Global Warming Linked to Plant, Animal
Extinctions," Climate Home, December 20, 2016. http://
www.climatechangenews.com/2016/12/20
/global-warming-linked-to-plant-animal-extinctions/.

Science and Environment, "What Is Climate Change?" BBC
News, November 14, 2016. http://www.bbc.com/news/
science-environment-24021772.

Tom Yulsman, "Heading into the Summer, Arctic Sea Ice Is in Bad Shape," *Discover Magazine*, May 5, 2017. http://blogs. discovermagazine.com/imageo/2017/05/05/arctic-sea-ice-is-in-bad-shape/#.WVZkMYjys2x.

Websites

Climate Central
http://www.climatecentral.org

This site provides news about the battle against global warming. It shows how science and many people are making positive changes and advancements to create a better environmental world.

NASA: Global Climate Change
https://climate.nasa.gov

The National Aeronautics and Space Administration is heavily involved in combatting the effects of climate change. Its site gives news and features about the global issue while promoting possible solutions.

Save the Earth Foundation
http://www.savetheearth.org

News and videos about saving the planet for animals and people are featured on this website. The organizations seeks to raise consciousness about the problems of global warming and climate change.

INDEX

Powder River Basin, 45, 74
Pruitt, Scott, 7, 43, 45, 46

R
renewable energy, 45, 46, 49,
    55–56, 62, 63, 64, 67, 68,
    69, 89

S
sea level rise, 6, 34, 57, 81,
    89–90, 94, 95
Social Cost of Carbon, 42, 47,
    48, 55
solar power, 46, 62, 85, 89, 94,
    97–98

T
Tam, Laura, 64
Trump, Donald
    denial of climate change, 6,
        43, 45, 50, 54, 58
    repealing environmental
        policies, 7, 40–41, 42, 46,
        47–48, 52, 54, 60–64, 94,
        95
    support of coal industry, 41,
        44, 55–56, 89, 93, 94
    withdrawal from Paris
        Agreement, 40, 54–55,
        86, 89, 90, 92, 93
tsunamis, 6, 14–18, 92

U
UK adaption plans, 37
UK climate projections, 35–37
US environmental policies,
    7, 40–48, 49–50, 52, 54,
    57–58, 61, 63, 85–86, 90
US Supreme Court, 45, 48,
    52–53

V
Vietnam, 67

W
wind power, 46, 50, 62, 63, 68,
    85, 89, 94
World Bank, 81